TEACH YOURSELF BOOKS
BADMINTON

FRED BRUNDLE

TEACH YOURSELF BOOKS
ST PAUL'S HOUSE WARWICK LANE LONDON EC4

First printed 1959
Second edition 1970
This impression 1972

ISBN 0 340 05518 9

*Made and Printed in Great Britain for The English Universities Press, Ltd., London
by C. Tinling & Co. Ltd., Liverpool, London and Prescot*

PREFACE

BADMINTON as a game is virtually without professional coaches, except for lawn tennis instructors filling in spare winter-time: and its hard-working honorary coaches are few and far between considering the enormous growth of the game in the nineteen fifties.

Fortunately it is a game which can be self-taught, more easily than any other racket game. If you try, good results are surprisingly quickly obtained.

This book is intended mainly for beginners, but many who have drifted into the game and picked it up, faults and all, as they have gone along will find in it a refresher course. It will pay good dividends in a better understanding of how to do what, where—and when.

One recommendation I do make most earnestly. Do not borrow this book for a fortnight and try to teach yourself badminton in that short time. It can't be done. Buy or borrow it for a longer period and assimilate a section at a time. Build up your game, stroke by stroke, over three months at least, or a full season of six months if possible. Take every opportunity for practice; turn up at your club on those shocking nights when the bad weather has kept down the numbers. You will feel the benefit of this "hastening slowly" in your second season. You will avoid that loss of initial enthusiasm felt by many a too-quick learner.

And *please*—enjoy yourself! For a few it is a serious pursuit. For thousands it's sheer fun. However you play it, it is still only a game, invented and developed for your pleasure and recreation.

FRED BRUNDLE

CONTENTS

ACKNOWLEDGMENTS

The author and publishers express their thanks to

E. B. Choong

C. T. Oon

H. I. Palmer

F. N. S. Creek

and

W. L. Steel

for expert advice on various parts of the text; and to Heather Ward, now Mrs. Nielsen, for her assistance with the instructional photographs. The Laws given in Chapter 3 are included by courtesy of the International Badminton Federation and the section in Chapter 3 headed "Hall Suitable for Badminton" is by courtesy of the Badminton Association of England and is reprinted from their Annual Handbook. The Recommendations to Umpires in Chapter 13 are included by permission of the Badminton Umpires' Association of England. The photograph of Erland Kops facing page 145 is reproduced by permission of Central Press Photos Ltd.

ILLUSTRATIONS

Photographic Illustrations

Line Illustrations

Measurements in these illustrations are quoted in feet (') and ("), and in metres.

CHAPTER I

HOW TO START

THE purpose of this book does not differ from the others in this series. It is to instil in you, the reader, the desire to teach yourself a game, the game of badminton. Once the interest and enthusiasm is aroused, people teach themselves anything, from Anthropology to Zen. By means of a few general interest chapters I hope to arouse or re-kindle *your* interest, by means of the action photographs to let you see how the champions make their shots, by providing you with all possible knowledge of the Rules, strokemaking and simple tactics to make it possible for you to teach yourself a game which will last you a lifetime. For this is perhaps badminton's greatest virtue. It can be played by young and old, by large and small, by girls and boys, by men and women, all on more or less equal terms. Strength is no criterion with the ultra-lightweight racket and shuttlecocks which are the tools of this delightful trade.

There are many—and it will do us no credit to deny it here—who think they cannot learn games from a book. It is usually the case that they are the type of person who can learn nothing from a book. But the vast majority of us are taught from an early age in just this manner—from a book. If one can learn so many things this way at school and college and evening class, then why not a game? Why not badminton?

The beginning of badminton is the co-ordination of hand and eye. To show you how one man began, here is a quotation from a book by Frank Devlin (Ireland), a former famous professional. It is from "Badminton For All", first published in 1932 and now, unfortunately, out of print:

"My earliest recollections of the game are hitting an old shuttle against my bedroom wall with a very ancient racket. I must have been about 12 years old at the time, and was recovering from an operation to my foot, so that I could not move about much but had to make the shuttle return to me. I remember counting the number of times I was able to hit the bird and finding I could get up to 50 or 60 if I concentrated very hard and watched the bird very carefully, but it was really hard work. Then suddenly I found the secret whereby I could play the shuttle comfortably and easily and make it bounce back right across the room to me. The secret was to play with my wrist and not my whole arm . . . to bend my wrist back and snap it forward as I hit the shuttle. . . . After a while I pulled some of the feathers out of the shuttle so as to deceive myself as to its flight; and became proficient at playing round the pictures with a minimum of damage to them."

What a brave beginning!

Another famous English international, T. P. Dick (Northumberland and Cheshire), who made 21 appearances for England between 1921-1933 and whose play I can just recall, was another who favoured knocking a shuttle against the wall for practice. If you try it, use an old shuttle and an old wall, I would hasten to add. Although this may not appeal to the purist, I think it is more effective than practising in front of a mirror. Personally, I could never stand the sight of myself doing it all wrong!

But a word of warning if you try this wall practice. When you start to play on a court, do not overlook the follow-through, necessary on many strokes to give you a smooth action. Like the tennis ball on a length of elastic—excellent practice for close volleying and getting and keeping your eye on the ball—the short space of time available before the ball returns to you makes a proper follow-through impossible. It is much the same at badminton when the shuttle comes off the wall. You will have little time for anything more than wrist flicks and jabs. You would not be able to project the shuttle the length of the court. Follow-through is not nearly as important in badminton as it is in lawn tennis, where it is essential to stroke along the desired line of flight of the ball. The lighter shuttle will not stop long enough after the initial impact which you give it. But many badminton strokes require a degree of follow-through. In case you are not *quite* clear on the point, follow-through in our context is merely the conscious effort of not attempting to arrest the racket at contact or immediately afterwards.

In net-play, and in particular with the lady close to the net, a long follow-through is not desirable. For full-blooded smashes, for half-angle smashes and for clearing strokes both underarm and overhead from well back in the court they are both necessary and desirable, if you want your game to be fully effective and stylish.

Apart from playing an old shuttle off the wall, the low serve can be practised over a piece of cord stretched across a living room or garage at a height of five feet. You might think that this one stroke out of all those in the game is not worth such individual attention. Believe me, it is. It is without doubt one of the most important strokes to learn quickly and learn well. For the lady in mixed doubles play in particular, it is of paramount importance. There must be many instances where a lady has been included in a match team on the strength of this one stroke alone. The man takes the lion's share of shots in the popular up-and-back formation. If his partner has a good varied low serve, she will both win points directly with it and will also make her opponents put the shuttle into the air from where her partner can effectively kill it or at least take the initiative. This stroke is one of the few that *can* be practised in the home. It is well worth a few hours. If you can shave the top of the net with the shuttle at will, you will be a sought-after mixed doubles partner and you will have a formidable weapon in your armoury for all sections of the game. Theoretically, the serve is not an attacking stroke. But if you can keep your serve low enough and vary its direction occasionally, you can turn it into one, and can constantly catch your opponent off guard.

That brings us to a consideration of the actual flight of the shuttle. As the late Ken Davidson—the most famous professional player badminton has known—has remarked elsewhere, those who have not played the game or are new to it have the impression that the flight of a shuttle-cock is erratic. Perhaps it is because we use "thrown about like a shuttlecock" and similar phrases in everyday life to denote being tossed this way and that, like a feather in a high wind. It is just not true. In still atmosphere, a shuttle will behave in exactly the same manner every time when hit at a given strength in a given direction. The champions rely on that to produce their best. They would be no more accurate than anyone else if this were not true. The shuttle will fly fast when you hit it hard, slowly when you stroke it softly. Whatever the speed of the shot, you must remember there is in badminton still a target area—the floor.

It is this slowness of flight which is so deceiving. It means that beginners are very soon able to enjoy rallies with each other. It makes badminton one of the easiest games to pick up quickly, at any rate in its bare essentials. But do not delude yourself because the shuttle passes back and forth over the net twenty times before it touches the floor that you know all about the game. Change your beginner opponent for me, and I will end the rally with you after one stroke. Put me—an experienced club player—at the opposite end of the court to Eddy Choong, the Malayan champion, and we may have exactly the same result.

(I have played singles against Choong. Although I have won *hands*, I have failed to score a point! As I knew he had frequently beaten international players 15-0, 15-0, I was not unduly dismayed).

It is these variations of flight speed which give the game its infinite variety. A famous lawn tennis player and writer criticised badminton some years ago on the grounds that there were only four strokes. There are not many more, when you come to add them up—the Clear, the Drop, the Smash and the Drive. But there are many, many kinds of drop shots and there are several kinds of smash, as our Danish and Malayan visitors have so ably demonstrated to us during the past few years. There are delicious cross-court net flicks and floating angled drops that find their way into no textbook but give enormous satisfaction—*and* the desired result when used sparingly. There are few basic strokes, true. But you will play badminton for fifty years (yes, fifty years as Mr. Stone of Warlingham did, from 1904-1954) and you will still find new strokes to add to your repertoire. It is the intention of this book to set you on that road, to show you how you can teach yourself either to play badminton or play better badminton.

You can begin, as indicated already, in the house or garage. You can continue in the garden; then, as a beginner, as soon as they have a vacancy, in one of the 10,000 clubs in the United Kingdom. First of all you will want to know the background to your game. The following chapter will put you in the picture.

CHAPTER II

FROM COUNTRY SEAT TO WEMBLEY ARENA

IT has been said that the game of lawn tennis owes much to "Real" or "Royal" tennis, the court game played by royalty and aristocracy during the thirteenth century and onwards. It the same way, badminton owes something of its origin anyway to shuttlecock and battledore. This began as a child's pastime, played standing still. The addition of a net made a game of it. It was first played standing still, then later with an unstipulated number of players on either side of the net to keep the shuttlecock in play. The necessity for running did still not arise.

The popular story which accounts for this sport being called Badminton is this. The Duke of Beaufort was entertaining guests at a house party at his country seat, Badminton Park, Gloucestershire, *circa* 1870. The rain drove them indoors and they sought entertainment there. They used the childrens' battledores and shuttlecock and stretched a cord across one of the large drawing rooms. It seems likely that it was played at some time in a room with doors opening inwards at the sides of the court. Credence is given to this theory because the shape of the badminton courts in use at that time remained pinched at the waist—4 feet narrower at the net than at the back of the court—until 1901. The actual room at Badminton Park is still in existence.

It is curious that a similar game was played at that time by officers of the Indian Army. In India it was called "Poona". The shuttlecock was not used originally but the womenfolk manufactured woollen balls on the sidelines. The wool was wound on a double disc of cardboard $2\frac{1}{4}''$ diameter, with a one-inch hole in the centre. The game became popular, and very nearly ousted croquet there, as lawn tennis was to oust croquet nearer home, at Wimbledon.

Again, up to five a side was the custom—and was the origin of "side-in" and "side-out" as preserved in the rules for many years. Accounts of the game as played at that time—around 1870—are non-existent. It is a matter of conjecture whether the Indian Army officers took the game from Badminton to Poona or brought it from Poona to Badminton. I favour the latter theory, if only because the original centres of this game—Folkestone, Teignmouth, Southsea, Bath and Southampton—were all centres for Services officers as well.

Major Clopton Wingfield mentions the game by name in his book "Sphairistike"—and his game, the forerunner to lawn tennis, was played outdoors on a waisted court. (For the keen student of racket games I recommend a visit to the British Museum Reading Room—you can get a day ticket on application on the premises—to read this fascinating little book, first published in 1874.)

The first Rules were drawn up by Colonel S. O. Selby, Royal Engineers, and published in Karachi in 1877. There were some unofficial rules published in England in the following year, believed to have been drawn up by a gentleman called Day, Racket Master at the Kennington Oval, who demonstrated the game for a fee of five guineas a night. It was not until 1887 that the available rules were revised by J. H. E. Hart, one of the pioneers of the game in England. They were revised again in 1890, foreshadowing the formation in 1893 of the Badminton Association. Colonel Dolby was the driving force—but his

efforts were premature to some extent. Few clubs
bothered to affiliate and the handful concerned in
founding the association went their own blissful way. It
was not until 1898 that the game really caught on, partly
because of the first open tournament, held at Guildford
in 1898. The Badminton Association decided to hold
their own open tournament the following year and
continued to do so thereafter. In 1902 the title was
changed to "The All-England Championships" both for
the past open tournaments and the future.

Badminton never looked back. The All-England
Championships have grown and prospered—but curi-
ously enough, have never been held outside London. It's
a wonder Manchester haven't had something to say to
that!

From the Drill Hall, Buckingham Gate, London, the
"All-England" moved to the Drill Hall, Bunhill Row,
London, E.C.1, thence to the most famous of its venues,
the Royal Horticultural Hall, Westminster, where it was
played in a pleasant garden party atmosphere until 1939.
When the Second World War broke out, it had already
been arranged to hold it where more spectators could
be accommodated—at Harringay Arena. The Championships duly transferred there after the war, in 1947, were
next staged at Earl's Court and finally, for the first time
in 1957, at Wembley Pool.

Wembley! It's a magic name for any sportsman. Later
in this chapter we will make an imaginary visit to the
Championships there.

But first, let us catch up on the changes in the
game from Guildford days to Wembley nights. The
court, as we have noted, has lost its waist and become
a standardised rectangle. Rackets have changed very
little, except that the wooden grip, popular until 1939,
has practically disappeared in favour of leather or a

substitute; and the shafts of wood may now be steel, metal alloy or fibreglass.

The biggest revolution has been the introduction of plastic shuttlecocks and the vast improvement of the feathered variety. From an odd collection of ill-assorted feathers to 16 perfectly matched, machine-tested, goose feathers: from a lump of rough cork to a regularly, precision-made piece of prime Spanish cork. The shuttlecock is no longer a hit-or-miss manufacture.

The plastic shuttle, like Colonel Dolby, came before its time. It is dealt with more fully in Chapter 4.

Now to Wembley, starting by taking the Underground to Wembley Park, then walking towards the famous silhouette of the beflagged Stadium. The Championships are not held there, but at Wembley Pool, adjoining it.

As it is almost impossible to obtain a ticket for a seat on finals day, we will assume that we have taken the precaution of getting a friend who was there on the Wednesday—opening day—to obtain tickets for us for the Friday evening. I have enjoyed some fine finals days. Yet, on the whole, I am sure the most memorable tussles take place on the Friday evening. On the Wednesday and Thursday of the meeting, the price of admission allows you to sit virtually where you will. The few hundreds attending these first two days can wander around almost anywhere—and up to six courts are in use. For a badminton fan this is most excellent value. The events are so arranged that you will see all the best players in action on these two days, even if not always fully extended.

By the time we pay our visit on the Friday, the number of courts in use has been reduced to three. We make our way through the wide passages surrounding the arena to

our seats. These are well placed to the right of the block
reserved for the Press. Beyond the Press section is another
popular institution at this venue, the arena restaurant.
Here at long tables directly overlooking one end of the
courts are places laid out for dinner. A full dinner is
served throughout the evening—and enthusiasts like
ourselves need not miss a moment of an exciting
match.

At a few minutes to six, two of the ladies involved in the
first semi-final appear from below the tiers, and are
closely followed by four men players. These three semi-
finals may be in progress at the same time—let's hope
they aren't *all* needle matches. As the men players belt
away at the shuttles, doing little exercises to limber up,
testing shuttles and generally trying to quieten the
butterflies that persist in flying around the stomachs of
even the most experienced players, a horde of well-
disciplined and knowledgeable officials descends on the
court under the generalship of an ex-international
player, an official of the Badminton Umpires' Association
of England. Many badminton players are lawn tennis
players as well. The kind of efficiency of organisation we
associate usually with the Wimbledon Championships is
evident to a large extent here at Wembley in the case of
badminton.

To club players like ourselves, these portable plastic
courts, perfect lighting and shuttles galore are a dream
come to reality. The officials lining the court might put
us off, but these stars are used to it all. In addition to
the umpire on his special seat high up above the net,
there are ten linesmen for a singles match and a service
judge.

The ladies involved in this opening match wait for a
little while as they are not scheduled to begin until 6.30;
the two men's matches begin in earnest at a few minutes

past the hour. On one court are Finn Kobbero (Denmark), the player the title holder Eddy Choong (Malaya) most fears, and his opponent Erland Kops (Denmark), an unseeded player who has had a comparatively easy path through to this semi-final round. But this is thought to be a certain win for Kobbero, so most eyes are focussed on the other match, Eddy Choong, a favourite of the English badminton public, against Joe Alston (United States), another popular player whose pleasant court demeanour during these meetings has endeared him to thousands.

You will notice as they finish their knocking up, that Choong has a fluent whipped backhand and moves like a cat across the court. Alston's style is in direct contrast. He is a smooth but slowish mover, but without particular grace and he tends to get under the shuttle, taking many shots with a round-the-head movement. During this knock-up, they alternate drives with smashes and drops. They do not trouble to probe each other's game. They have played each other a number of times before. Choong has a plan before he goes on court for any game. He is a law student, works his plan out in cold logic, and executes it with speed, stamina and accuracy. Alston is a fighter (in private life a Los Angeles F.B.I. man) and hopes to match Choong's stamina, take the edge off his speed and blunt his accuracy by maintaining a perfect length.

The lesson which the keen learner will acquire from watching this preliminary sparring is that a knock-up needs to be done with a purpose. Choong smashes two shots and both come off perfectly. He does not smash again: that shot is working. But a flick clear fell well out beyond the base line. This he does again . . . and again . . . and again—until it falls exactly on the base line. Then he nods approvingly and goes on to practise other strokes. This is how you should practise with a friend, as often as possible. Just knocking the shuttle into the air will prove nothing nor improve your game a jot. Sustained backhand clears with plenty of follow through will strengthen you on this wing, develop your accuracy where accuracy is harder to find. Another lesson to be learned is that cold muscles need warming up slowly. You are not like a milkman's electric float: press the button and away we go. You are more like a motor-car. After starting from cold, a warming-up period is needed, without full throttle. Once warm, you can strip your outer clothing and make your all-our efforts.

But to consider the actual match. The first few rallies remind us that this is to be a war of attrition. Both these players are superbly fit and conditioned to long matches. Choong appears to have things in hand in the first game, mainly due to his speed in putting down Alston's occasional weak shot. Alston is also presenting Choong with odd points by cutting things too fine with his drop shots. Instead of dropping just over the net, they are hitting the net cord and falling back into his court. At last Choong clinches the first game at 15-11. The not-unusual reaction then sets in and Alston runs up a lead in the second game before Choong realises that Alston is in fact increasing the pace, the tempo of the rallies, by more smashing. Alston takes this at 15-9 after 45 minutes tremendous, classic play. Now the pattern of the match emerges. Choong starts off the third game at a tremendous pace, smashing anything available to smash, eliminating error and flinging himself along the floor to scrape up impossible shots. He is rewarded by a healthy lead of half-a-dozen points, but here Alston's tactics suddenly reap a rich reward. Those wasted drops in the opening game are no longer wasted. His touch has suddenly become perfect, and he disguises the cross court-drop shots until the very last moment, leaving Choong no chance at all. As these bring him back to level pegging, he gives his opponent the full blast of his attack, smashing more vehemently, sometimes more accurately than Choong. A lesser player than the Malayan would have wilted and fallen back under this bombardment. But not Choong. Alston has hauled himself up to 13 all after an hour's desperate play and it is anybody's match. The very momentum Alston had gathered is to prove his undoing. Just too soon his smashes begin to lack 100 per cent accuracy. The game is set at 13-all. Two of his smashes hit the net at this score—and these two strokes virtually cost him the match, although 16 all is reached before Choong obtains the two points to give him an 18-16 win in the deciding game. What a match! So absorbing, indeed, that we have hardly noticed the biggest surprise of the Championships on an adjoining court, with the unseeded Kops playing above himself for the evening— and putting out No. 2 seeded player Kobbero. Nor indeed have we noticed the ladies' singles which has begun—and ended—on the court between the two men's events.

As the players come off court, Choong and Kops, the finalists for the following day, are besieged by photographers—and we sink back in our seats to get over the match ourselves. Who won the ladies singles, you ask? A look on the projected scores at the end of the arena indicates that the former All-England and American champion, Judy Devlin, has beaten Joe Alston's petite and charming wife, Lois, with comparative ease. We leave our seats to refresh ourselves at one of the many counters in the arena's wide corridors, in readiness for more sparkling doubles play. We feel we have already had our money's worth this evening, yet doubles matches to come include the top pairs of Denmark, (Kobbero and J. Hammergaard Hansen), Canada (Peter Ferguson and Dave McTaggart), England (Tony Jordan and Jack McColl) and the famous Malayan Choong brothers, Eddy and David, three times holders of this sought-after title.

After we have watched all this talent, we realise that a shuttlecock will do just about anything an expert player wants it to do . . . *no* shot is impossible to pick up . . . and that between the best, Deception is all. None of these great players relies on one or two match-winning strokes: all can vary their game to meet the demands of the moment—and all lose points if their concentration lapses.

We notice, too, that to some extent, certain players are born great. H. A. (Johnny) Heah, for example. He has a natural grace of movement, a steady temperament, and an uncanny eye for following a fast-moving object. How could he help but play well the game of badminton? He might have been the greatest player of all but for two things. His stamina was suspect (so I am told, but I never spotted the weakness myself)—and his studies of Architecture in London and Cambridge meant that he spent his time in England more in books than on court. During the first two years, he often tamed the ubiquitous Eddy Choong: during this, his last All-England Championship in those 7 years, he won the men's doubles title with Alston in a fast, breath-taking final against the Choong brothers, a great reward for a great player.

Other players—Alston is such a case, I imagine—need steady application and cool calculated play to make up for any natural deficiency of inherent talent to give the same results. All the players we have seen this evening have played a high standard of badminton. But I am sorry you missed Wong Peng Soon (Malaya), who turned professional last year. He played effortless singles. And if only you could have seen Dave Freeman, who played only once in England, in 1949. Even the grey-beards who remember the golden days of Sir George Thomas nodded approvingly at his error-free magnificence. Both had perfect footwork.

There are so many lessons to learn from watching these top players. This perfect length they maintain—you can practise that. The controlled backhand—you can practise that. Indeed, most of these points you so admire can be improved by the right sort of practice.

On the way back to Wembley Park Underground, we thank our lucky celestial stars we picked this evening to see the shuttle stars. We have seen badminton at its best. It gives us hope. We may not be able to·play like them—but we can certainly do better than we have done before.

But please do not confine your badminton "spectator-ship" to the All-England Championships. To be honest, although you will see the best badminton in the world there, you will not see badminton at its best. The smaller arenas where only one match at a time is in progress and you are closer to the court give you a better view of the finer points of stroke play. If you live in South London or Surrey and are keen to watch good play, enquire when the Wimbledon and Ebbisham (Epsom) Clubs are holding their tournaments. In North London you can see many internationals in action at county fixtures at Orion Hall, Stamford Hill. Indeed, at most county matches no admission, or a purely nominal fee, is levied and you will find these charged with friendly rivalry and keen excitement.

A study of the "Badminton Gazette" (the official organ of the Badminton Association of England, published from

81a, High Street, Bromley, Kent) gives lists of all Sanctioned Open tournaments and Championships, as well as the county fixture list. There is one big event near everyone's home.

The players we have described in this chapter were the stars of the nineteen fifties when this book was first published. A decade later the scene is very much the same, the crowd as large and enthusiastic but the names are different. The Malayans and Danes have been challenged by Indonesians, Germans and—particularly among the ladies—the Japanese.

The leading world-class players at the beginning of the seventies are Rudy Hartono and Darmardi (Indonesia), Tan Aik Huang and Tan Yee Khan (Malaysia), Borch, Walsoe and Pri (Denmark), Derek Talbot and David Eddy (England), together with the ladies, Hiroe Yuki and Noriko Tagaki (Japan), Minarni and Takahashi (Indonesia), and England's Gillian Gilks, with the doubles players Margaret Beck, Julie Rickard, Linda Spencer, Charlotte Lindsay and Bridget Cooper.

These are the players who will battle for the honours. But competition at the top was never keener. It makes for a very high standard of badminton.

China should soon emerge as a powerful badminton country. Two of her players, Tang Hsien-hu and Hou Chia-chang, successfully toured Canada in 1971. They played unaggressive doubles but were unbeaten in all their singles matches. Jamie Paulson was the only Canadian player to take even a game off them.

CHAPTER III

THE LAWS AND THEIR INTERPRETATIONS

LET no doubt remain in your mind: it *is* possible to teach yourself badminton. Many famous players admit to this, several in the top flight as this book is being written.

But if you, the reader, are really serious in your intention to follow the title of our book, the first essential is to study the Laws of Badminton (I prefer to call them the Rules.) The trouble with Rules is this. They have to be worded in lawyer-like terms to avoid double meanings and interpretations. Then they are a bore to read. There is no doubt about it at all, only about one in five players in any ordinary badminton club has ever read the rules.

But you are going to teach yourself badminton. You must have a sound knowledge of them to start that job at all. So here they are, as they have been drawn up and amended over the years, first by the Badminton Association, later by the International Badminton Federation. The four Interpretations at the end are official. The comments are my own.

THE LAWS OF BADMINTON

As revised in the year 1939 and adopted by
The International Badminton Federation.
Subsequently revised up-to-date.

Court

1. (*a*) The Court shall be laid out as in the following

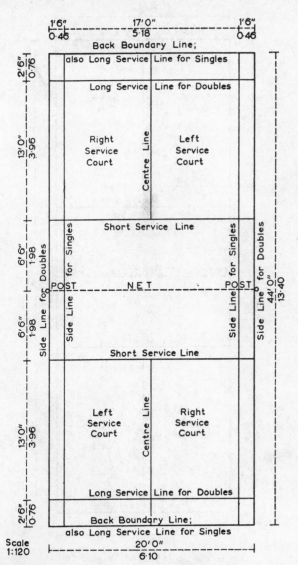

Fig. 1. The Court (doubles). Diagram (A).

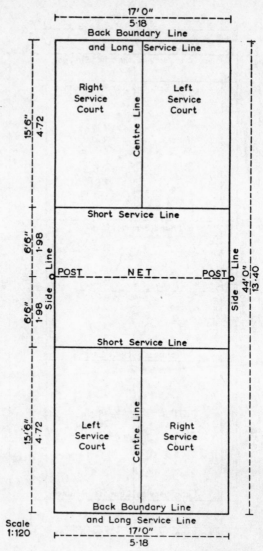

FIG. 2. The Court (singles). Diagram (B).

Diagram "A" (except in the case provided for in paragraph (b) of this Law) and to the measurements there shown, and shall be defined by white or yellow lines or, if this is not possible, by other easily distinguishable lines, $1\frac{1}{2}$ inches wide.

In marking the court, the width ($1\frac{1}{2}$ inches) of the centre lines shall be equally divided between the right and left service courts; the width ($1\frac{1}{2}$ inches each) of the short service line and the long service line shall fall within the 13-feet measurement given as the length of the service court; and the width ($1\frac{1}{2}$ inches each) of all other boundary lines shall fall within the measurements given.

(b) Where space does not permit of the marking out of a court for doubles, a court may be marked out for singles only as shown in Diagram "B". The back boundary lines become also the long service lines, and the posts, or the strips of material representing them as referred to in Law 2 shall be placed on the side lines.

Posts

2. The posts shall be 5 feet 1 inch in height from the floor. They shall be sufficiently firm to keep the net strained as provided in Law 3, and shall be placed on the side boundary lines of the court. Where this is not practicable, some method must be employed for indicating the position of the side boundary line where it passes under the net, e.g., by the use of a thin post or strip of material, not less than $1\frac{1}{2}$ inches in width, fixed to the side boundary line and rising vertically to the net cord. Where this is in use on a court marked for doubles it shall be placed on the boundary line of the doubles court irrespective of whether singles or doubles are being played.

Net

3. The net shall be made of fine tanned cord of $\frac{5}{8}''-\frac{3}{4}''$

mesh. It shall be firmly stretched from post to post and shall be 2 feet 6 inches in depth. The top of the net shall be 5 feet in height from the floor at the centre, and 5 feet 1 inch at the posts, and shall be edged with a 3-inch white tape doubled and supported by a cord or cable run through the tape and strained over and flush with the top of the posts.

Shuttle

4. A shuttle shall weigh from 73 to 85 grains, and shall have from 14 to 16 feathers fixed in a cork, 1 inch to $1\frac{1}{8}$ inches in diameter. The feathers shall be from $2\frac{1}{2}$ to $2\frac{3}{4}$ inches in length from the tip to the top of the cork base. They shall have from $2\frac{1}{8}$ to $2\frac{1}{2}$ inches spread at the top and shall be firmly fastened with thread or other suitable material.

Subject to there being no substantial variation in the general design, pace, weight and flight of the shuttle, modifications in the above specifications may be made, subject to the approval of the National Organisation concerned.

(a) in places where atmospheric conditions, due either to altitude or climate, make the standard shuttle unsuitable; or

(b) if special circumstances exist which make it otherwise expedient in the interests of the game.

(The Badminton Association of England has approved the use of modified shuttles (e.g. plastic, nylon, etc.) for play in England.)

A shuttle shall be deemed to be of correct pace if, when a player of average strength strikes it with a full underhand stroke from a spot immediately above one back boundary line in a line parallel to the side lines, and at an upward angle, it falls not less than 1 foot, and not more than 2 feet 6 inches short of the other back boundary lines.

Players

5. (*a*) The word "Player" applies to all those taking part in a game.

(*b*) The game shall be played, in the case of the doubles game, by two players a side, and in the case of the singles game, by one player a side.

(*c*) The side for the time being having the right to serve shall be called the "In" side, and the opposing side shall be called the "Out" side.

The Toss

6. Before commencing play the opposing sides shall toss, and the side winning the toss shall have the option of:—

(*a*) Serving first; or

(*b*) Not serving first; or

(*c*) Choosing ends.

The side losing the toss shall then have choice of any alternative remaining.

Scoring

7. (*a*) The doubles and men's singles game consists of 15 or 21 points, as may be arranged. Provided that in a game of 15 points, when the score is 13-all, the side which first reached 13 has the option of "Setting" the game to 5, and that when the score is 14-all, the side which first reached 14 has the option of "Setting" the game to 3. After the game has been "Set" the score is called "Love All," and the side which first scores 5 or 3 points, according as the game has been "Set" at 13- or 14-all, wins the game. In either case the claim to "Set" the game must be made before the next service is delivered after the score has reached 13-all or 14-all. Provided also that in a game of 21 points the same method of scoring be adopted, substituting 19 and 20 for 13 and 14.

(*b*) The ladies' singles game consists of 11 points. Provided that when the score is "9-all" the player who first reached 9 has the option of "Setting" the game to 3, and when the score is "10-all" the player who first reached 10 has the option of "Setting" the game to 2.

(*c*) A side rejecting the option of "Setting" at the first opportunity shall not be thereby barred from "Setting" if a second opportunity arises.

(*d*) In handicap games "Setting" is not permitted.

8. The opposing sides shall contest the best of three games, unless otherwise agreed. The players shall change ends at the commencement of the second game and also of the third game (if any). In the third game the players shall change ends when the leading score reaches:—

(*a*) 8 in a game of 15 point;

(*b*) 6 in a game of 11 points;

(*c*) 11 in a game of 21 points;

or, in handicap events, when one of the sides has scored half the total number of points required to win the game (the next highest number being taken in case of fractions). When it has been agreed to play only one game the players shall change ends as provided above for the third game.

If, inadvertently, the players omit to change ends as provided in this Law at the score indicated, the ends shall be changed immediately the mistake is discovered, and the existing score shall stand.

Doubles Play

9. (*a*) It having been decided which side is to have the first service, the player in the right-hand service court of that side commences the game by serving to the player in the service court diagonally opposite. If the latter player returns the shuttle before it touches the ground it is

to be returned by one of the "In" side, and then returned
by one of the "Out" side, and so on, until a fault is made
or the shuttle ceases to be "In Play". (*Vide* paragraph
(*b*).) If a fault is made by the "In" side, the server's hand
is out, and as the side beginning a game has only one hand
in its first innings (*vide* Law 11), the player of the opposing side in the right-hand service court now becomes the
server; but if the service is not returned, or the fault is
made by the "Out" side, the "In" side scores a point.
The "In" side players then change from one service
court to the other, the service now being from the left-
hand service court to the player in the service court
diagonally opposite. So long as a side remains "In"
service is delivered alternatively from each service court
into the one diagonally opposite, the change being made
by the "In" side when, and only when, a point is addded
to its score.

(*b*) The first service of a side in each innings shall be
made from the right-hand service court. A "Service" is
delivered as soon as the shuttle is struck by the server's
racket. The shuttle is thereafter "In Play" until it touches
the ground, or until a fault or "Let" occurs, or except
as provided in Law 19. After the service is delivered, the
server and the player served to may take up any positions
they choose on their side of the net, irrespective of any
boundary lines.

10. The player served to may alone receive the service,
but should the shuttle touch, or be struck by, his partner
the "In" side scores a point. No player may receive two
consecutive services in the same game, except as provided
in Law 12.

11. The side beginning a game has only one hand in its
first innings. In all subsequent innings each partner on
each side has a hand, the partners serving consecutively.
The side winning a game shall always serve first in the

next game, but either of the winners may serve and either of the losers may receive the service.

12. If a player serves out of turn, or from the wrong service court (owing to a mistake as to the service court from which service is at the time being in order), and his side wins the rally, it shall be a "Let," provided that such "Let" be claimed or allowed before the next succeeding service is delivered.

If a player standing in the wrong service court takes the service, and his side wins the rally, it shall be a "Let", provided that such "Let" be claimed or allowed before the next succeeding service is delivered.

If in either of the above cases the side at fault loses the rally, the mistake shall stand and the players' positions shall not be corrected during the remainder of that game.

Should a player inadvertently change sides when he should not do so, and the mistake not be discovered until after the next succeeding service has been delivered, the mistake shall stand, and a "Let" cannot be claimed or allowed, and the players' positions shall not be corrected during the remainder of that game.

Singles Play

13. In singles Laws 9 and 12 hold good, except that:—

(a) The players shall serve from and receive service in their respective right-hand service courts only when the server's score is 0 or an even number of points in the game, the service being delivered from and received in their respective left-hand service courts when the server's score is an odd number of points.

(b) Both players shall change service courts after each point has been scored.

Faults

14. A fault made by a player of the side which is "In" puts the server out; if made by a player whose side is "Out", it counts a point to the "In" side.

It is a fault:—

(a) If, in serving, (i) the shuttle at the instant of being struck be higher than the server's waist, or (ii) if at the instant of the shuttle being struck the shaft of the racket be not pointing in a downward direction to such an extent that the whole of the head of the racket is discernibly below the whole of the server's hand holding the racket.

(b) If, in serving, the shuttle falls into the wrong service court (i.e., into the one not diagonally opposite to the server), or falls short of the short service line, or beyond the long service line, or outside the side boundary lines of the service court into which service is in order.

(c) If the server's feet are not in the service court from which service is at the time being in order, or if the feet of the player receiving the service are not in the service court diagonally opposite until the service is delivered. (*Vide* Law 16.)

(d) If before or during the delivery of the service any player makes preliminary feints or otherwise intentionally baulks his opponent.

(e) If either in service or play, the shuttle falls outside the boundaries of the court, or passes through or under the net, or fails to pass the net, or touches the roof or side walls, or the person or dress of a player. (A shuttle falling on a line shall be deemed to have fallen in the court or service court of which such line is a boundary.)

(f) If the shuttle "In Play" be struck before it crosses to the striker's side of the net. (The striker may, however, follow the shuttle over the net with his racket in the course of his stroke.)

(g) If, when the shuttle is "In Play", a player touches the net or its supports with racket, person or dress.

(h) If the shuttle be held on the racket (i.e. caught or slung) during the execution of a stroke; or if the shuttle be hit twice in succession by the same player with two strokes; or if the shuttle be hit by a player and his partner successively.

(i) If, in play a player strikes the shuttle (unless he thereby makes a good return) or is struck by it, whether he is standing within or outside the boundaries of the court.

(j) If a player obstructs an opponent.

(k) If Law 16 be transgressed.

General

15. The server may not serve till his opponent is ready, but the opponent shall be deemed to be ready if a return of service be attempted.

16. The server and the player served to must stand within the limits of their respective service courts (as bounded by the short and long service, the centre, and side lines), and some part of both feet of these players must remain in contact with the ground in a stationary position until the service is delivered. A foot on or touching a line in the case of either the server or the receiver shall be held to be outside his service court. (*Vide* Law 14 (*c*).) The respective partners may take up any position, provided they do not unsight or otherwise obstruct an opponent.

17. (a) If, in the course of service or rally, the shuttle touches and passes over the net, the stroke is not invalidated thereby. It is a good return if the shuttle having passed outside either post drop on or within the boundary lines of the opposite court. A "Let" may be given by the umpire for any unforeseen or accidental hindrance.

(b) If, in service, or during a rally, a shuttle, *after*

passing over the net, is caught in or on the net, it is a "Let".

(*c*) If the receiver is faulted for moving before the service is delivered, or for not being within the correct service court, in accordance with Laws 14(*c*) or 16, and at the same time the server is also faulted for a service infringement, it shall be a let.

18. If the server, in attempting to serve, misses the shuttle, it is not a fault; but if the shuttle be touched by the racket, a service is thereby delivered.

19. If, when in play, the shuttle strikes the net and remains suspended there, or strikes the net and falls towards the ground on the striker's side of the net, or hits the ground outside the court and an opponent then touches the net or shuttle with his racket or person, there is no penalty, as the shuttle is not then in play.

20. If a player has a chance of striking the shuttle in a downward direction when quite near the net, his opponent must not put up his racket near the net on the chance of the shuttle rebounding from it. This is obstruction within the meaning of Law 14 (*j*).

A player may, however, hold up his racket to protect his face from being hit if he does not thereby baulk his opponent.

21. It shall be the duty of the umpire to call "Fault" or "Let" should either occur, without appeal being made by the players, and to give his decision on any appeal regarding a point in dispute, if made before the next service; and also to appoint linesmen and service judges at his discretion. An umpire's decision shall be final, but he shall uphold the decision of a linesman or service judge. This shall not preclude the umpire also from faulting the server or receiver. Where, however, a referee is appointed, an appeal shall lie to him from the decision of an umpire on questions of law only.

Continuous Play

22. Play shall be continuous from the first service until the match be concluded; except that (*a*) in the International Badminton Championship and in the Ladies' International Badminton Championship there shall be allowed an interval not exceeding five minutes between the second and third games of a match; (*b*) in countries where climatic conditions render it desirable, there shall be allowed, subject to the previously published approval of the National Organisation concerned, an interval not exceeding five minutes between the second and third games of a match, in singles or doubles, or both, and (*c*) when necessitated by circumstances not within the control of the players, the umpire may suspend play for such a period as he may consider necessary. If play be suspended the existing score shall stand and play be resumed from that point. Under no circumstances shall play be suspended to enable a player to recover his strength or wind, or to receive instruction or advice. Except in the case of any interval already provided for above, no player shall be allowed to receive advice during a match or to leave the court until the match be concluded, without the umpire's consent. The umpire shall be the sole judge of any suspension of play and he shall have the right to disqualify an offender.

(The Badminton Association of England has not sanctioned any interval between the second and third games of a match.)

Interpretations

1. Any movement or conduct by the server that has the effect of breaking the continuity of service after the server and receiver have taken their positions to serve and to receive the service is a preliminary feint. For example, a server who, after having taken up his position

to serve, delays hitting the shuttle for so long as to be unfair to the receiver, is guilty of such conduct.

(*Vide* Law 14 (*d*).)

2. It is obstruction if a player invades an opponent's court with a racket or person in any degree except as permitted in Law 14 (*f*).

3. Where necessary on account of the structure of a building, the local Badminton Authority may, subject to the right of veto of its National Organisation, make bye-laws dealing with cases in which a shuttle touches an obstruction.

Hall Suitable for Badminton
WITH RECOMMENDATION FOR LIGHTING

The following are the main requisites in a hall suitable for one or more Courts.

HEIGHT

Not less than 25 feet over the middle of the court.

SPACE AROUND COURT

Where there is only one court there should be at least 3 feet clear all round it. Where two courts are side by side, they should be 4 feet apart.

BACKGROUND

This should be uniform and may be almost any colour except white or cream, the shade being sufficiently dark to give good contrast with the white shuttle. A very dark background is not essential for reasons given below. (See LIGHTING.)

FLOOR

The surface should be smooth but unpolished, and of a sufficiently dark shade, preferably of brown or green, to show up the white marking lines.

MARKING

The lines should be white and non-glossy. Most paintmakers now supply a hard-wearing non-reflecting white paint.

POSTS

Those on a metal base screwed to the floor on the sidelines are most satisfactory, but where these cannot be used, posts with well-weighted bases will hold the net to its regulation height satisfactorily.

LIGHTING

(1) *Daylight.*—This should if possible come from above through sky-lights. In a hall without sky-lights, light should only be admitted through windows at the sides of the court. Any windows facing either end of the court should be completely screened.

(2) *Electric.*—Many forms of electric lighting are now available and one which shows the white shuttle in its true colour should be used.

The minimum number and size of ordinary lamps recommended will vary slightly with the type of surroundings, but where the walls, floor and ceiling of a hall are not unduly dark in colour a fair minimum of lighting is obtained by hanging a line of six 150 watt lamps at each side of the court parallel with the side lines. They should be at a height of 13 feet above the floor and 2 feet outside the net posts. The line containing the six lamps should not exceed 6 feet in length, *i.e.*, 3 feet on each side of the net.

If a flat white-painted (non-glossy) reflecting board of approximately 8 feet by 2 feet is placed vertically behind each line of lamps it will be found that six 100 watt lamps can replace the 150 watt lamps and will give results almost equal to the above and with less glare.

Pearl lamps are more satisfactory than those with clear or obscured types of glass.

Any type of shade or reflector which forms a deep hood around the lamps will increase the light in the centre of the court, but these are not recommended because they cut off the light from the ceiling and back of court.

NOTE.—The above lighting data is given as a guide for an economical form of producing sufficient lighting for play without causing undue eye·strain. When considering the many other forms of lighting, careful consideration should be given, particularly before installing the fluorescent type when, unless a minimum of eight tubes are placed on each side of the court, results may be found inadequate.

Comments on the Laws

Law 1 deals entirely with the marking and dimensions of the court, Laws 2 and 3 with Equipment and Law 4 with the shuttlecock—officially described as a shuttle. It is by this shortened name that it is generally known, or, in the vernacular, "the bird". You may have noticed at a preliminary reading that, as with lawn tennis, no size or weight or material is laid down for your racket. (Squash rackets, on the other hand, legislates on this matter, due to the proximity of the players to each other in the court.) Theoretically, you can play badminton with a cricket bat or a tennis racket. In practice, the shape and size of rackets has become standardized.

Law 4 was carefully redrafted some years back to give the plastic shuttle official sanction as it was obviously about to be used all over the world. The last paragraph of Law 4 has come under heavy fire on many occasions. You will have noted that it deals with the pace of a shuttle and says that "it shall be deemed to be of correct pace when a player of average strength strikes it with a full underhand stroke from a spot immediately above one back boundary line in a line parallel to the side lines, and at an upward angle, it falls not less than one foot and not more than 2 ft. 6 ins. short of the other back boundary line". A panel of judges would be needed to decide which of your club members was of average strength, whether their stroke was a *full* underhand stroke, and whether it was struck in a line parallel to the side lines: and a tape measure to measure exactly where it fell. In half the church badminton halls in England, too, it is impossible to find the room behind the base line to swing the racket sufficiently for this idealistic test. Better by far to leave it to the manufacturers to test the shuttles at their factories. If they prove too fast (or slow) for your hall, you will know after five minutes play. And you can then ask your dealer to change them.

Law 5 rules out the varied numbers of players on both sides of the net permitted in grandfather's day, Law 6 deals with the Toss. This somewhat archaic heading disguises the fact that nowadays the Toss (originally one presumes of a coin, although this object is not specifically mentioned) is carried out almost invariably by spinning the racket as in lawn tennis and calling rough or smooth to the spin. If you win the Toss, where there is some advantage in a particular end of the hall—many have a stage with dark coloured curtains and this background provides the better end to be facing—choose your end. If you or your doubles partner are good servers, choose "Serving first" (as it is only the server who can score at all), but if you are nervous starters and cannot see much advantage in either end, choose "Not serving first"—and pass the buck to your opponents.

One further comment on this Rule. If you win the toss and elect "Not serve first", your opponents then have the choice of any alternative remaining. BUT NOT ALWAYS BOTH. If they choose to serve, the choice of ends again passes to you. If they choose ends, you insist

they serve as well as your choice as winners of the Toss
was "Not to Serve".

Law 7 deals with Scoring. Although the doubles and
men's singles games consist of 15 or 21 points, 21 points
are rarely played nowadays, never in open tournaments
and championships. The "Setting" system is quite simple
when you get used to it but will repay a second reading if
you are a beginner. It should be carefully noted that a
side rejecting the option of "setting" at the first opportunity is not debarred from "setting" if the chance arises
again: and that no setting at all is allowed in handicap
games. (The times I've seen this done!)

Law 8 deals with the length of the games and number
of games in a match, Law 9 with Doubles play, by far
the most widely played branch of the game. This is
because about 2,500 of the 3,000 affiliated badminton
clubs in England are one court clubs.

Laws 9-12 show you clearly the course of doubles play,
Law 13 deals briefly with singles. Law 14 is worth very
particular study. It deals with Faults. Laws 15-21 are
General Laws and clarify some that have not fully
explained themselves. You must be careful when receiving service to allow a shuttle which is going to fall
short to hit the ground. There is no other way of proving
that it was indeed short. Resist the temptation to hit the
very short shuttle back to the server before it has struck
the ground. If you do, he can claim the point, quite
correctly. You will note that in Law 17 an umpire may
give a "Let" for any unforeseen or accidental hindrance.
If anything untoward happens in your club play or league
match played without an umpire, all should quickly
agree on a "Let". It will save a lot of argument.

So much, then, for the Laws of Badminton. On the
whole they are straightforward and once you have begun
to play, simple to follow.

The Badminton Umpires Association of England, formed in 1954, is the guardian of these laws in England. A number of suggestions for the amendment of the old Laws and the evolution of new ones have been and will be put to them and to the Badminton Association of England; but these Laws are now approved by the International Badminton Federation in the interest of uniformity throughout the badminton-playing world. Because of this it would be very difficult to get any substantial amendment to the present Laws without world support.

Clarifications of Law 16 were given, however, quite recently and are included in "Recommendations to Umpires" (1957) under heading No. 32. The I.B.F. was asked to rule if certain foot, toe and heel movements were breaches. They ruled that none were.

CHAPTER IV

EQUIPMENT

BEFORE you actually play any game you need the time, the place and the equipment, which may or may not include special clothing. We will assume you have both time and place for the moment and turn our attention to equipment and clothing. If you are going to teach yourself badminton, there will be a minimum: or you may be lucky and be able to get the best of everything, so we will also examine that fortunate situation.

The Racket

Most important is the badminton racket. Now while the Laws do not lay down anything at all about the size or substance of a racket, over the years rackets have become more or less standardised. My pre-war rackets are in point of fact a shade larger than my post-1946 purchases, although the same weight.

As many of the readers of this book will be tennis players, I would like to make it clear straight away that it is my considered opinion that the initial selection of a racket for badminton is much less important for this game than for tennis. So much of badminton is wrist work, so little variation exists in weights, that the only two considerations worth considering are balance and thickness of handle.

To define a standard racket, I would say that it should weigh about 5 ozs., be about 26 inches in length, have a wooden frame, single piece or laminated, in ash, beech or hickory and have a shaft of wood, steel or fibreglass, with a handle about $3\frac{3}{4}$ inches in circumference.

If you are at school or college there may be club rackets for you to try. If you are at home, you will doubtless start your badminton life with a racket passed down from your parents or other relatives. But if you are buying in a shop or store or have any choice in the matter, my advice is to try first for a comfortable grip. If you have a small hand, you will need a small grip or handle: if you are a big fellow, you can well afford a stouter one. The "feel" of a badminton racket—you will get this by making a series of imaginary strokes at the thin air—is most important. As I will explain later, you have to make friends with your racket. For this it must *feel* right, whatever other virtues or vices you are to discover in it. You want it to feel like an extension of your arm, a large, friendly helping hand.

If you are buying a cheap one from a store—and several of the stores have real bargains in this line, manufactured in large quantities for them by the best firms, *incognito*— test it by flexing it. A well-made racket will bend evenly from the grip to the top of the head. If the racket bends only from the throat up towards the frame, the shaft is stiff and the head in all probability too weak for hard hitting.

It has been estimated that half the cost of the racket is in the frame, half in the stringing. For this reason alone, I recommend—if you are buying—a good frame. You can have many re-strings on a good frame before it finally shatters. I still have the racket I bought with my first prize voucher more years before 1939 than I care to remember. I have also a beautiful new fibreglass-shafted racket which I use a great deal. This was presented to me by my local club members in 1956, after 10 years as their captain. But I find I cannot completely desert my old friend, a Prosser, almost unobtainable nowadays.

It is difficult to know how to test the stringing. I have heard that the tightness of the string can be determined by placing the end of the handle against the face bone just under the ear and gently brushing the strings with the backs of the fingers, with the finger nails. A satisfactory tone is said to be C sharp at middle C on the piano, with D or D sharp well suited to most average players. Since I do not know a note of music, this does not help me at all! I can tell you that the tighter strung the racket is, the less long it will last but the greater the initial speed it imparts to the shuttle. Tournament players have tightly strung rackets—with several stringings a season. Club players can have less tightly strung rackets and these will normally last a whole club season quite comfortably. Many club players have slightly thicker gut and go for 3 or 4 years at a time without re-stringing, but this depends largely on the standard of their play.

Gut or nylon? Nylon wears very well and is to be recommended for club play. My reserve racket is nylon-strung in its third season at this time. Good gut is undoubtedly the best stringing, has longer life, and more resilience, but is more susceptible to dampness. The enthusiast for the finer strokes in the game always plumps for gut, but I recommend you to try both for yourself.

Whatever type of racket you finally use on court, do keep it in a press in a dry place. The cupboard in the church hall annexe is *not* good: a corner of your wardrobe at home is. And when you put your racket away for the summer months, remember to smear the strings with gut reviver. If there is none handy, rub on some mutton fat.

Shuttles

The second necessity before you start to play will be some shuttles. When you consider that the whole game of badminton hinges on the flight characteristics of the shuttle, you will understand how important they are, much more than at ball games because of the greater accuracy required at many points of the game.

For many years the feathered shuttle, originally more barrel-shaped, was universally used, although the search for a substitute for the fragile goose feather began in the 1890's. These substitutes were mainly papier-maché, then celluloid, later plastics, polythene and nylon.

Mr. W. C. Carlton, of Carlton Shuttlecocks Ltd., has been the man behind the development of the plastic shuttle. This development from an admitted "substitute" shuttle to the International Nylon, a cork-base plastic production suitable for the highest class of play, has been over a mere decade. I have no doubt that the new generation will take these new shuttles in their stride, for the cost of *beginning* badminton must be kept down, and this is how to do it.

Plastic shuttles are always used for outdoor play nowadays. They form a valuable export to Europe, America and, latterly, to Malaya and the Orient. Up to 1957, nearly all plastic shuttles originated from the firm of Carltons. In the 1957-58 season, competition arrived in the shape of R.S.L.'s Nash Plastic, developed in the United States and manufactured in England.

Both these manufacturers were kind enough to provide me with standard models of these for test purposes. The tests I carried out both privately and in local clubs with the following results. The table below is *not* a table of merit but merely indicates how much badminton you can expect from the various shuttles *at ordinary club standard*. Top class feathers cost (at the time of writing) about £3·00 per dozen, club quality about £2·50 per dozen, and plastics from £1·50 down to £1·10 a dozen, according to type.

Feather	RSL No. 1 Tourney	. . .	1½ hours
	RSL Silver Feather	. . .	1 hour
Plastic	Carlton International Nylon .		3 hours
	Carlton Club Nylon	. . .	3 hours
	Carlton Polythene	. . .	4 hours
	RSL Nash Polythene	. .	4 hours

Most of the defects of the plastic shuttle have now been overcome. The earlier models were all particularly difficult for accurate short service and close net play. Some of the later models are also poor in this respect. Critics have also alleged that you cannot "kill" a plastic. For club play, when longer rallies prolong the enjoyment and excitement of the game, this does not seem a particularly serious fault.

In 1952, Law 4 was altered to allow use of plastic shuttles, the later types undoubtedly enjoying most, if not all, of the flight characteristics of the feathered variety. I have dealt with the matter of shuttles in some detail because there still exists a certain amount of friction between the "fors" and "against" with plastics. At the time this book is written, the plastic shuttle is in wide use in the North of England, the Midlands' Leagues and Youth Clubs and similar organisations everywhere. In the South, there exists strong prejudice against it. An evening's badminton of four hours can be had comfortably with one of these plastic shuttles for under two shillings. The equivalent cost in feathered "birds" (bearing in mind that the cheaper grades do not last as long as the dearer) is not less than ten shillings. But where cost is not overriding, most badminton players of a good standard prefer feathers. That I think sums it up as fairly as possible.

For our purposes, for learning the game, plastic is best because of its durability. But try to get hold of some discarded club feathers—most clubs will be only too glad to give you a tube of them—in order to use both for the rather rough treatment our "teach yourself" method requires.

In 1957 the Badminton Association of England issued a special notice regarding the speed of modern shuttles, which it considered had become too slow. The diagram is reproduced below, and the text of the notice read:—

"The Council of the Badminton Association of England is of the opinion that the average speed of shuttles presently used throughout the country is 9-12 inches less than is permitted by the Laws of Badminton. In consequence of the foregoing decision a directive is hereby issued that if any player, competing in any sort of match, should insist on the correct pace shuttle he must have it."

"Law 4 states:—A shuttle shall be deemed to be of correct pace if, when a player of average strength strikes it with a full underhand stroke from a spot immediately above one back boundary line in a line parallel to the side lines and at an upward angle, it falls not less than 1 foot and not more than 2 feet 6 inches short of the other back boundary line."

"In order to fulfil this requirement when testing the pace of shuttles, the front foot must be placed *immediately behind* the back boundary line, as shown in the attached diagram. The back boundary line should *not* be straddled."

By order of the Council of The
Badminton Association of England.

On the subject of nets and net posts I will only observe that the majority I have seen in the smaller clubs need a boy scout to erect them. They are replete with ropes and pulleys and tightening devices, mostly quite unnecessary to support a light net. If you are ever in the position of

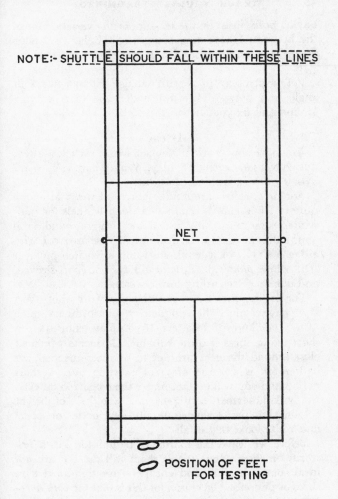

NOTE:- SHUTTLE SHOULD FALL WITHIN THESE LINES

NET

POSITION OF FEET
FOR TESTING

Fig. 3. Testing the pace of a shuttle.

buying posts, insist on the self-supporting variety. One of the best sets I have seen consists of tubular steel posts fitting into cantilever solid steel legs. These sell at about £16.

For garden play, drive with a sledge hammer two stout angle iron posts (6 ft.) just under one foot into the ground and fix your net to these.

Dress

You have now provided yourself with a racket, shuttles, and have somewhere to play. What shall you wear? Whatever it is, it should be white.

For men, shorts are almost universal wear, although quite a few diehards retain their long flannels for mid-winter wear, especially useful for sitting-around in if your hall is inclined to be draughty. These are worn with either a singlet or a tennis shirt and a woollen pullover (still white, *please*); it is useful to have one short-sleeved, and one long, according to the weather.

For ladies, shorts are occasionally worn, but short skirts have retained their popularity, some ordinary, some of the type known as skaters. If you play tennis, then a short tennis dress is quite suitable. Garments which fit close around the neck are not to be recommended, for badminton is a game of great exertion over a short period and you will get hot under the collar too quickly. Many ladies wear cardigans or "woollies" of bright colours, but pastel shades usually look better on court and white looks best of all.

Before we leave the matter of badminton kit, a few words on shoes. Your tennis shoes will do, but are not ideal. Better by far—and cheaper—are thin-soled gym shoes or plimsols. The reason for this is that the considerations which apply for tennis are not valid for indoor badminton. For tennis, you require a firm platform from which to play your strokes, a grip on the court because of the sometimes pronounced body swing and a cushion for your feet for long periods of time on a hard, often hot surface. But now consider your badminton requirements. They are very different. You make many of your strokes on the move, some as you weave your way about the court, you require your feet to slide a little, or to swivel as you rapidly change direction, and your enclosed feet are only in contact with a smooth wood floor, occasionally sprung. I have often thought the ideal badminton shoe is a bare foot; and I well remember a Danish girl in our club some years ago who, when the game got to a very exciting stage, took off her shoes. She showed remarkable mobility when she did this.

Ready now then? Ready for anything? That's the spirit! A good badminton player is always a little aggressive. Let's begin that way, shall we? Remember you can smash the shuttle with all your might and main! It still won't break a window or do anyone a serious injury. So smash it, will you?

The Court

The last essential is a court on which to play. For the beginner, this is the biggest difficulty of all. Lawn tennis offers many public courts in recreation grounds, squash rackets the use of club courts at certain times. But public badminton courts? You will have to go a very long way to find one at all in England!

If you can play even a little, the problem is not insurmountable. There are many clubs which have a small number of vacancies every season for *players*. If you apply to one of these, you will be asked down to see the club— and for them to see you—on one of their early season evenings. If you show the least promise, you will be accepted, for as we have remarked elsewhere, it is a game picked up—to a certain modest standard—very quickly indeed. But what if you are an absolute beginner? I suggest that you continue to read this book with the utmost care, and begin badminton in your garden in the summer.

For garden badminton, a full size court is not absolutely necessary. The game has its limitations in the British climate, and you will not be able to perfect the touch strokes or the low service. But for the general run of the game, scoring, the overhead clears and the drives, it is very good practice indeed. You can play with a woollen ball, with a plastic outdoor shuttle or with a discarded feathered shuttle, weighted by inserting in the cork base from the inside a small screw. By the time you have had a few hours of play like this, with or without a net, you will be striking the shuttle cleanly and consistently. When you apply for membership of the local club, you will then be a player!

But you insist on joining a club during the winter? There is but one place for you to practise—indoors. This can be done, either in a boxroom or a garage, by standing some feet from the wall and striking the shuttle against it. You have read an account of Frank Devlin's first attempts at shuttle smashing in Chapter 1. A number of experts have recommended this wall play for beginners, both to quicken the reflexes and to ensure you start with that flexing of the wrist, that supple twist and turn which are so essential to the game of badminton.

CHAPTER V

THE GRIP—THE USE OF THE WRIST— FOOTWORK

The Grip

"Genius does what it must, talent what it can."

The Lawn Tennis Correspondent of *The Times* is credited with this shrewd observation. He sometimes writes on badminton. We will assume you are, like me, no genius but that you have some talent. With that talent we will do what we can.

You are now ready to take your racket in your hand and go out on to the court. You will want to know how to hold the racket. Your natural grip—and I will say here and now I much prefer the word grasp—may be quite all right. But let us check it. (We will assume you are right-handed: if you are left-handed, please reverse most of these instructions.) Try it this way.

Hold the racket at the neck in your left hand with the palm of your hand flat against the racket and your first three fingers flat against the strings pointing up the racket head. Now offer the handle to your other hand. Close you right hand firmly but not tightly around the handle, the first finger slightly spaced from the second as this first finger is not really involved in the grip. Check that the leather rim at the extreme end of the racket handle does not project beyond the hand but remains within the palm. (In this way you will use the maximum length of your racket and extend your reach.) How does that feel? You have the normal forehand grip suitable for a variety of shots.

An alternative method of checking your grip is to hold the racket at the throat in the left hand again, then place your *right* hand flat against the strings on the opposite face. Now slide your hand down the racket handle until it reaches the grip and grasp again, firmly, but not tightly. You will arrive at the same position by a slightly different method. You will be "shaking hands" with the racket handle. This is an excellent thing to be doing. The racket is your best friend on court: in singles especially you need to be on the very best terms with it in order to defeat the enemy, your opponent.

While this shake hands grip is ideal for most shots on the right hand or forehand side of the body, both underhand and overhead, many players alter their grip slightly for certain backhand or net shots. The experts differ greatly on this point and I find it difficult to be dogmatic about the question.

Sir George Thomas, one of the game's great players of the past, kept the end portion of his thumb resolutely turned down and used exactly the same grip for practically all forehand and backhand strokes. Yet he acknowledged that some of the most formidable players of his Golden Age of badminton pointed the thumb up the handle for backhand strokes. Nevertheless he considered it definitely wrong to turn the handle at all, a fault (he thought) inherited from lawn tennis. Eddy Choong also thinks there are generally speaking too few strokes necessitating a changed grip to make it worth while as a normal practice. David Choong is another player who executes most high backhands with a forehand grip.

But Sir George and Eddy and David were to some extent unique. You and I are not. It is possible we shall find many of the backhand strokes easier to make accurately if we change our grip slightly, the handle turning slightly, the racket head turning away from the body and the thumb pointing up the "flat" of the handle grip.

The late Ken Davidson, as fine a coach as the modern game has produced, taught this. He thought the thumb acts as a lever and adds control and power, helping to guide the racket forward to meet the shuttle and helping to add impetus to the racket head. Ian Palmer, a well-known Surrey coach, says: "I think that the thumb certainly should point up the flat of the grip for the backhand shots, especially those taken overhead and when taken off the left foot. You will find this gives much more power to the final flick of the racket, held loosely at the beginning of the swing of the stroke."

If you are teaching yourself badminton, you will want as little alternative advice as possible. You will not want any confusion in your mind. So my advice is to use the thumb up method, suitable for the majority of players of both sexes. If you have an exceptionally flexible and strong wrist, you will soon know it; and will know that this will suffice for all normal strokes.

You have the racket grip lodged in the palm of your hand then. Comfortable? Check on these points.

1. Are your fingers bunched together? Relax. Open them a little. With a tight grip you will never cultivate that precious "touch", the feel of the racket through your fingers, especially the index finger.

2. Is your grip too tight? Confess it if it is. I estimate that 9 out of 10 beginners grip too tightly—and 4 out of 5 experienced club players. This fault, so easily corrected at the beginning, can tauten your wrist and arm muscles so that you lose all control, even to the point of contact with the shuttle.

The Use of the Wrist

This leads us on to the use of the wrist, unimportant at

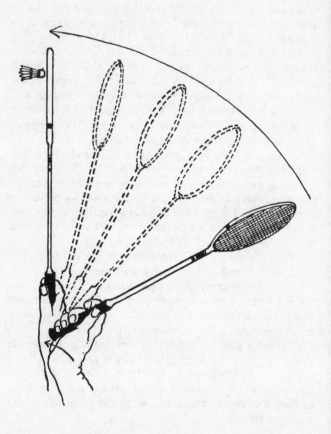

Fig. 4. Cocking the wrist. The movement with racket.

THREE GREAT
MALAYAN PLAYERS

Upper Left:
EDDY CHOONG

Upper Right:
WONG PENG SOON

Left:
G. T. OON

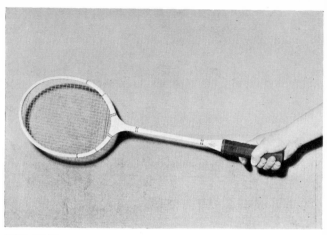

THE GRIP

FOREHAND (HEATHER WARD)

BACKHAND (HEATHER WARD)

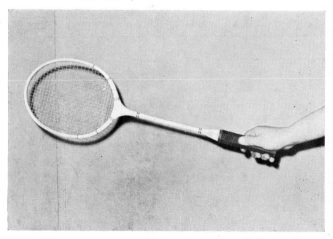

lawn tennis except in the locking of it, of only moderate importance at squash rackets, BUT OF PARAMOUNT IMPORTANCE AT BADMINTON.

In some ways the actual cocking of the wrist at badminton is one of the most difficult movements to teach a beginner. (See illustration.) It is perhaps best demonstrated by taking in the hand a limp object, not a rigid racket. Take out your pocket handkerchief for example. Hold the two ends in your hand, stand an old shuttle or a plastic mug on the table in front of you and strike the object sideways, to knock it off the table. Note how the wrist cocks, then unwinds itself at the moment of impact imparting a flicking movement to the folded handkerchief. It is the same action as whipping a top.

The backhand cocking movement is similar. Set up your target again and flick it down. Whenever I see a play on the stage or television where the Knight pulls out a gauntlet from his belt and slaps the villain around the face, I always nudge one of my children (potential badminton players) and say: "That's it! That's the backhand, Sir Lancelot."

Practise that for a while until you have the idea. If it's near Christmas or a birthday and there are balloons about, better still. These are ideal for backhand practice with just your hand.

Once you have assimilated the cocking action of the wrist, think of the rotation of it for a moment. The shuttle is so light that the slightest swivelling movement of your wrist will send it flying in a totally different direction from the one that was expected. This is particularly useful on service, when you want to keep your opponents guessing until the last possible moment. Examine your hand and wrist for a moment. Cock it and rotate it a dozen or more times. What a piece of engineering it would be in steel! They are developing

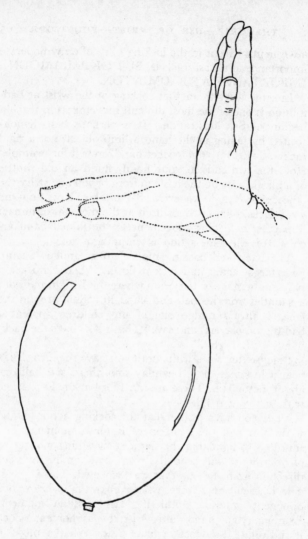

FIG. 5. Wrist-cocking practice with a balloon (forehand).

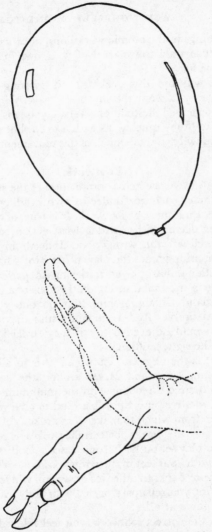

Fig. 6. Wrist-cocking practice with a balloon (backhand).

such things in the atomic workshops, of course—yet they reproduce only the marvel of your own natural wrist movements.

You will use this cocking and rotating movement whenever you want the shuttle to travel fairly fast to a pre-determined destination. When you wish it to fall away, to "die" quickly, as with a drop shot close to the net, you will avoid too much of this movement.

Footwork

I shall leave the actual production of the strokes until we consider each one under its own heading. The next consideration must be footwork. It is true, of course, that a clever player with a strong wrist action can function quite well off the wrong foot. Indeed, in many fast championship games the players have to: I have seen an international star player retrieving to perfection three smashes in succession sitting on the floor of a court at the All-England Championships. But no one will pretend this is desirable. And I am quite sure these players of genius would be even better if they stroked with their feet in the right position.

What is the object of footwork? It is to allow you to move your body and racket around the court in the various desired directions with the minimum of fuss and bother, the least effort possible: and to give you the best platform from which to make your stroke. You will know if your feet are wrong for certain strokes as soon as you begin to play seriously. In some cases a good swing at the shuttle with your feet in the wrong position will leave you flat on your back. In other instances you will feel as if you are tearing yourself apart, or that your body was not made for the game at all.

With the correct footwork, you feel relaxed and confident that you can put the shuttle where you want it—

with no fuss or bother at all. With the feet in the right position you will be able to use the weight of your body correctly, distribute it equably in relation to the stroke and the force of the stroke you are attempting.

But, you ask: "How do I cultivate correct footwork?" This must depend, in the first instance, on what style of

FIG. 7. Position of feet for a normal forehand stroke.

footwork you are going to adopt. The first school thinks you should be poised on the balls of your feet ready to skip about the court with a number of short steps in any given direction. You finish up ready to make the stroke with your feet in similar positions to those on the tennis court. The weight of your body is supported on the foot furthest from the net for forehand strokes, is transferred to the left pivot foot as you make the stroke. Your body will swivel round on the left foot and your right foot will

FIG. 8. Position of feet for a normal backhand stroke.

come forward automatically if there has been any swing. For the backhand power strokes the reverse applies. Your right foot is nearest the net, your left, back foot has the weight on it at the beginning of the stroke. The weight is transferred to the right foot, the pivot in this case, and your left foot comes forward and round as you complete the swing.

But another powerful and convincing school of thought maintains that you can cover the whole of the singles court from your central base position in two strides. You do not (it argues) therefore need all this scurrying about. And you *can* cover it, you know. Two strides and you can reach the four corners of the singles court quite easily. Try it!

If this is valid in singles, how much more valid in the smaller area of court which is your preserve in the doubles game. You will take the forehand underhand strokes off your right foot, the overhead forehand as previously described, swivelling on your left foot. But for the overhead backhand, you will find you can take these shots quite easily off the left foot, using a thumb-up grip. From the backhand corner this has a decided advantage. Your right foot does not need to come across the body as much as with the first method described (as it has not the weight of the body on it and you are not swivelling on your right foot at all). You can therefore keep both net and opponent in view, which is sounder strategy than turning your back on them.

I have often been asked why, at racket games, the right foot needs to come across the body at all for power strokes. The answer is that your body—especially the chest—needs to be eliminated. If you do not do this, then in many strokes your chest will block your arm as it attempts to go back and you will lose power in your stroke. Try making a backhand drive straight up the court with your feet in the forehand position and you will see what I mean.

Before we leave the subject of footwork, there is the small complication (to the beginner) of the swivelling movements. These are aids to fast footwork and mobility.

A pivot on the ball of the foot nearer to the shuttle will help bring the other foot into movement and position. It also starts the body movement in the right direction and helps save that split second, such an important feature of badminton.

The beginning of good footwork is to be off those two flat feet. No offence is meant here. But I feel the injunction to be "on your toes" is apt to be misleading—if not practically impossible for some persons of considerable stature. I know a county men's doubles player who must weigh at least 16 stone: but his footwork is perfect. If I could travel about on my toes I might have danced at Sadlers Wells. As it is, I have torn one leg tendon at badminton, one at tennis and am as flat footed as you find them. This doesn't stop me from being reasonably mobile (I like to think). Try to move about, with knees flexed, on the balls of your feet—as soon as the shuttle is in play. This way you will avoid becoming rooted to the spot.

The Malayan school often liken badminton footwork to boxing footwork. With two contestants of equal merit at either game, the one with good footwork wins. He catches the one with poor footwork off balance—he is in racket terms "wrong-footed"—and at that most vulnerable moment, his opponent strikes to win the fight or to win the rally. Paul Whetnall is an example of a modern player with a boxer's footwork, Roger Mills another.

Your feet are the beginning of your source of power. Power is only needed in half the strokes of badminton, but it is particularly required in the Smash, of course. Your power will be unleashed from your feet, will course through your coiled body and run along your unflexed arm to find its outlet at the moment of impact just after you have uncocked your wrist, the last link in the chain.

In cold print, this may sound cumbersome. In point of fact, when you have perfected the movement, it will be like a ripple across water. But it will give the shuttle that clean, crisp impetus you will come to recognize as a good stroke.

CHAPTER VI

TEACHING YOURSELF TO SERVE—TO RECEIVE SERVICE—TO KEEP CONTACT

Teaching Yourself to Serve

It was Robert Lynd in *Essays On Life and Literature* who observed that almost any game with almost any ball is a good game. The thought is equally applicable to badminton, whose sort of ball is a feathered one. It is such an easy game to pick up once you have mastered the initial co-ordination of hand and eye—and shuttle.

This is the first snag you will run into in teaching yourself badminton. You will have difficulty in serving. You will have difficulty because you will be making things difficult for yourself. You will probably be throwing the shuttle upwards and trying to hit it over the net as the shuttle comes down.

When you are beginning, there is no need for this preliminary throw, a feature of old-time badminton, when the type of service was known as a toss service. Try it this way.

Stand with your feet about eighteen inches apart in an easy, relaxed position. Your left foot will be in advance of your right (as it is a forehand stroke) and you will be side on to the net or to your opponent in the opposite court. In doubles, your position in your own court should be about a yard behind the short service line and certainly not more than a yard from the centre line. From the left hand court, you should be as near as possible to the centre line. (In singles, since the pivot position is the centre of the court, you will always stand as close to the centre line as possible.)

When you are all set in this position, pause for a second

to see what your opponent is doing, what position he occupies in court. This is important and I do not hesitate to introduce into your serving at this early stage what is basically tactics. For it is what you notice then that will determine in many cases what serve you will now execute. If your opponent is crouched menacingly near the net, a high service over his head would be in order. But we will assume the receiver is waiting mid-court, in an orthodox position. You will serve short and low.

This low, short service is the basic doubles serve and is the best for you to learn first. No power is needed and the other serves can be grafted on to it quite naturally. Now please, *please* take it slowly at this juncture. This is the one moment in our imaginary game that you are in complete control. You have the shuttle, you have a good platform, your racket is under control, you are quite still—and you are the only one who can score at that moment. Why hurry? Time enough later in the game, when the rally has got going.

Make your delivery as simple as possible in these two easy movements. Hold the shuttle out in front of you in your left hand a little below shoulder height: take your racket arm back not more than twelve inches, but with your wrist cocked. You are ready, poised. Hold it!

Now just open your hand and drop the shuttle, at the same time swinging your right arm forward in an easy pendulum movement. If all goes well the racket should meet the shuttle at about arm's length in front of the body and project in gently over the net. It may fall short of your opponent's service court. If it does, try it again but quickening the movement of the arm or wrist slightly just before impact. More likely, you will find yourself hitting it too strongly so that it flies up into the air over your opponent's head, in such a position that he can either knock it down or even kill it. You will therefore lessen the speed of the racket head at contact to ensure a lower flight line for your service shuttle. This can be done by cocking the wrist less, relying on arm movement to impart "travel" to the shuttle.

What if you do not make contact at all? This can happen all too easily, especially if your game has been tennis and you are quite new to badminton. Persevere for a while. Practise on your own in the garage or garden. After two or three dozen strokes you should be making contact quite nicely. If it still will not come, try making no backward movement of the racket arm at all, nor cocking the wrist. You will be simply dropping the shuttle two feet in front of the racket, and lessening the margin of error. As soon as you make contact, take your racket back a few inches at a time and begin to cock your wrist. After a very short while you will arrive at the point of an easy forward swing into the shuttle.

It must be stressed again here that missing or mis-hitting the service is usually caused by hurrying the stroke, seldom by taking it too slowly.

When you have mastered this short service action—the refinements of placing it into different parts of your opponent's court can wait for the present—you will be ready to execute a high doubles serve. You will use exactly the same swing. You will *appear* to be doing exactly the same thing right up to the actual striking of the shuttle. At the last minute you will increase the movement of your arm and possibly your wrist and will there-fore strike the shuttle harder. It will sail up over your opponent's head. If left to fall, it should drop within a few inches of the long service line.

It cannot be too fully emphasised that there should be no difference in the preliminaries for these two services. Badminton's cornerstone is Deception. You must try to keep your opponent guessing. Either of these services can be directed to different parts of the court, or to your opponent's body (if that is a direction in which he has shown himself vulnerable).

On the low service, the *trajectory* of the shuttle is particularly important. Ideally, the flight of the shuttle should reach its highest point on the server's side of the net. It should fall more steeply after crossing the net and, if left to drop, should be within an inch or two of the short service line.

For the high doubles service, the trajectory of the shuttle is of less importance. It must clear your opponent's outstretched racket arm and should drop well back in the court. This service is rather easier to execute and should be used while you get the feel of the game. But a tall opponent with a good smash will relish the opportunity to warm up on *his* strokes, so mix short serving into your game as early as possible.

When you have practised the low, short service and the high doubles service (the first you can try in the garage at home over a piece of cord stretched across five feet from the ground: the latter will have to be done on a proper court or in the garden), try the third type of service. This is the angled drive serve, called by the Malayans the "shooting" service.

This serve is executed with a similar swing to the other serves, but sometimes from a position further to the right of the service court. The object is to shoot the shuttle (from the right hand service court) on to your opponent's backhand. It can be a very awkward serve to receive, particularly if the receiver is not equipped with a round-the-head smash. This serve is rarely tried from the left hand court for in this case it shoots on to your opponent's forehand; but shot wide, it can occasionally be used as a surprise stroke with great effect.

The following diagrams illustrate the four most com-

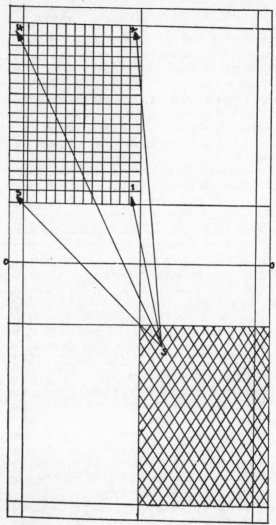

FIG. 9. Four doubles serves from the right-hand court.

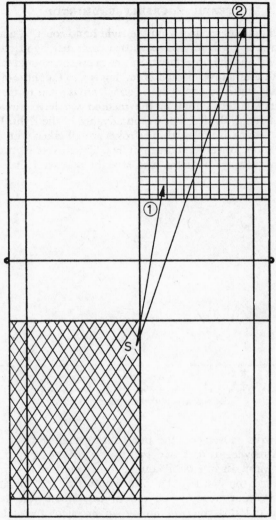

FIG. 10. Two doubles serves from the left-hand court.

mon doubles services from the right hand court, 1, 2 and 3 low, 4 a lob service—and two basic left hand court serves: and the trajectory the three main ones should take.

An alternative method of serving is also taught to-day. It has much to commend it and I advise you to try it. You will recall that in the method we have already considered, the left foot was in advance of the right. For this alternative method the strokes are all taken with the right foot forward, off the right foot. The strokes are made nearly always with the arm straight and with little or

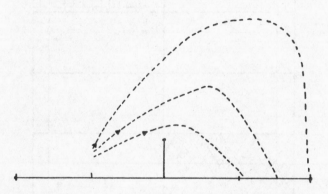

FIG. 11. Three service trajectories. (1) the low serve, (2) the high doubles serve, (3) the high singles serve.

no wrist movement, the fine control coming from the arm movement itself and the pivoting of the body from the waist. Its one disadvantage for a beginner is that it requires the shuttle to be thrown outwards and forwards on to your outstretched racket. But when you have mastered this you will find it an excellent method of service, capable of many variations. It is equally effective from either court, and in mixed doubles should always be taken from as near the centre line as possible.

One further point on serving. Your position when serving in doubles games will depend to a large extent on your partnership, whether you are playing a strict back-and-front formation, or a side-by-side—or may depend even on your partner's strength (or weakness). You will understand this more after reading about tactical play later in this book. For the moment, remember that a good position is about a yard behind the short service line and close to the centre line. You can vary your position sometimes in men's and ladies doubles, but not in the mixed doubles. This variation need not be by more than a foot-or-two at the most—but it will prevent you from serving along the same channel each time with the consequent telegraphing of your intentions to your opponents. In any case the position you take up in court for serving should never indicate that you are about to do a certain service. There is a school of thought that maintains that one should *always* take up the same position, but I find an occasional change helpful.

Almost all I have said so far concerns serving in doubles. In the singles game, the position is much simpler. You will almost invariably toss up the highest accurate serve you can to drive your opponent as far back in court as possible, leaving him with a shuttle dropping down perpendicularly. If your aim is singles, this high serve to a length must be regularly practised. It is no use unless it is accurate to within six inches of the long service line. The short serve is used occasionally, merely as a variation. No other services are used in singles.

It is sometimes said that at badminton the server starts at a disadvantage in that he has to serve underhand. On the other hand, you can only score when you are serving—and for a brief moment, you are dictating what course the game shall take. This may have unsuspected advantages if you are able to force a certain reply. Whatever else your serve may lack at first, please make sure it has *purpose*. If it has that, then you are well on the way to turning a defensive stroke into an offensive one.

To Receive Service

Now let us cross the net and get on to the receiving end of these three types of service we have been considering. As all the serving strokes put the shuttle up into the air, we will assume that as receiver we have the offensive: that is to say, by and large, we should be in a position to hit most of them down.

The server, as we have seen in our study of the Laws, must hit all serves not higher than waist level, and with no part of the head of the racket higher than any part of the server's hand holding the racket (Law 14: see illustration). As receiver you *should* be able therefore—if quick enough!—to meet all serves above waist level. To do this you will need to adopt an alert position, a stance from which you can move quickly in any direction.

This business of an aggressive stance need not be over-emphasised. Some of the best players I have seen, both British and Malayan, hardly trouble about it at all. It will depend largely on the personality of the player. Personally, I like to adopt a threatening attitude—but then I always was a bit of a bully! But seriously, I can see no object in a player of sweet unruffled, gentle demeanour crouching in the service court, suddenly assuming the guise of a tiger. On the other hand, if the player is aggressive in his or her game throughout, he will fall naturally into an aggressive stance for this phase of the game, the receiving of the service. In match play, the sight of a man crouched ready to pounce on their short

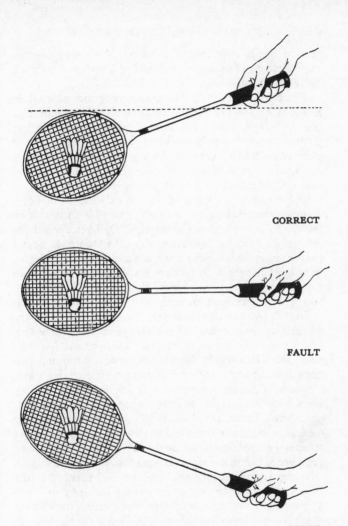

CORRECT

FAULT

FAULT

FIG. 12. The racket and the hand at service. Law 14.

service should it be loose, has certainly a strong psychological effect, especially on ladies. But however you stand,
be ready for anything.

The best position to be in to receive service at doubles
is about a yard behind the short service line again. But
this will depend on what sort of person you are, what
formation you have adopted with your partner and your
partner's ability. Your ability to deal with overhead
shots, your speed of foot and your reflexes all have to be
taken into consideration. A young, speedy player can
afford to come in close to the short service line and
threaten the receiver, almost jump down his throat as he
serves. He has the speed to skip quickly back should the
service fly over his head. On the other hand, a slower
player must stand more than a yard back in order to
guard against the high service: it will always be easier to
run forwards than backwards. Wherever and whenever
you receive service, wait with your knees slightly flexed.

So that you can receive the service on the forehand, try
to take up your receiving position near the centre line
when you are in the righthand court, about 3-4 feet
away from it when in the lefthand court. Assuming you
are adopting some sort of crouching position, which foot
forward? I favour weight on the left foot, leaning forward with your racket a little higher than, and behind,
your head. From this position you will be equally ready
for immediate movement either forward, to jump a short
service, or backwards, to deal with a high service over
your head. But many right-handed players receive service
with the right foot forward. This enables them to strike
the shuttle nearer to the net, shortening the distance it has
to travel on its return (and therefore reducing the chance
of error) and lessening the time of flight.

Now although your weight will be on the left foot as
you wait for the server to strike the shuttle, you will

begin to move as soon as you have determined the direction and trajectory of his stroke. Should you decide that the shuttle will fall somewhere in front of you, you must go to meet it. There is a strong tendency among players new to the game to wait for the shuttle to come to them. It never does. The flight characteristics are very different from those of a ball. The trajectory curve dies away quickly. It is most important you reach the shuttle and strike it for your return stroke when it is as high in the air as possible. This has particular significance when receiving an accurate short service. The later you leave the shuttle, the lower is the position from which you will have to strike it and the longer you give your opponent to take up a position to pounce on *your* return to his (allegedly) defensive stroke, his underarm service.

These considerations apply to doubles. In receiving in singles, remember your aggressive stance is wasted—you almost have time to say a prayer while the shuttle is coming down sometimes—and you must not move before the shuttle has been struck. The singles court is longer and narrower than the doubles. As far as receiving service is concerned, about mid-court is as good a place to wait as any: there is no point in getting in close to rush a short service for if you are in that position you may be sure you will be served only with high serves.

To Keep Contact

You will begin to understand now how to serve and how to receive service. It is here, before we go on to show you the four basic strokes, that I want to impress upon you an essential feature of badminton—keeping contact.

This is not one of the Principles of War of which you may have heard; it is a vital element in badminton. The contact you must strive to keep is with the shuttle. It is especially important in badminton because within reason there is no shot you cannot reach. You can hurl yourself across court so as just to get your racket to the shot whipped down your sideline. You can throw yourself towards the net to scoop up what looked an impossible one—and you will get it if you try hard enough—or you can leap into the air to claw down that "bird" which was intended to fly away over your head.

Now many of these strokes will not be worth the candle tactically. But all are worth a try when you are learning the game. This is in order to convince yourself—and if you later convince your opponent at the same time, so much the better—that no rally is lost until the shuttle has actually reached the ground.

While you are learning the basic strokes and long before you have perfected stroke-making, get the habit of intercepting your racket in the flight of the shuttle whenever possible. If you have to chase it remember the flight characteristics of a shuttle. It starts off at no end of a speed, suddenly slows down, with brakes on, then drops to the floor at no ground speed at all. So it pays to chase it. You stand your best chance of overtaking it as it begins to slow down rapidly—at the end of its flight.

While it is important for a net player to know what to take and what to leave, it is also important that he develops this contact game. The successful and correct interception of a shot may not gain a point in itself. What it so often does is speed up the rally sufficiently to force an error from your opponents or to wrong-foot either or both of them.

As an experiment, I once saw two players of county standard beat a good club pair solely on interception. They promised they would not actually stroke a shot, only intercept and place. They kept their promise—and won narrowly.

So much of doubles badminton is placing and angling

the shuttle on a downward path, that keeping contact is all-important. Lose contact and you will begin to run about all over the court with the one object of scooping-up the shuttle—to start you on another leg of the race. In this way you will never have the initiative and will not therefore be able to mount any sort of attack.

Remember this: in any rally where the shuttle is not being cleared, the point to regain the initiative is at *the moment the shuttle crosses the tape*. With the thumb up backhand grip, you can strike the shuttle at that moment: the rules allow for your racket to follow through into your opponents' court, providing you do not hit the net. That is the moment for the lady in the mixed doubles partnership to hit the shuttle down. That is the point at which she will—Keep Contact.

CHAPTER VII

THE CLEAR—THE SMASH—THE DROP—
THE DRIVE—NET STROKES

The Clear

The Clear, sometimes called the Lob, is by far the most widely used stroke in the game. The High Clear is defensive, the Low Clear more usually an attacking stroke. For all overhead forehand clears the motion used is exactly similar to that of throwing a ball.

The clears will all be taken overhead when you are in a position to do so, or underhand if you are not. The high clear is probably the easiest stroke in the game to execute. But it needs practice to give you a good length to within a few inches of your opponent's baseline—and this need for accuracy cannot be stressed too much. If you clear short you are asking for trouble. If you clear falls mid-court, it will be dealt with most severely by one of your opponents: you will have put it just where he or she likes it. When you have progressed and are playing top class badminton, you will find it is—literally—only a few inches which is the difference between good high clears and bad high clears. (I have assumed, in this chapter, where the doubles game is concerned, that you are playing the back-and-front formation.)

Your underhand clear will be made in many cases in a similar position to the high service. The overhead clear on the forehand is the same stroke taken overhead, but you ensure that you hit the shuttle at the highest point you can comfortably reach and that you hit it up with your arm straight at point of contact. You must govern also

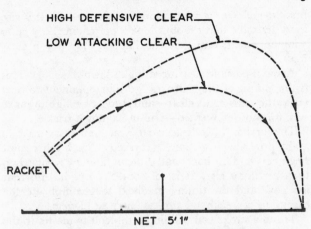

HIGH DEFENSIVE CLEAR

LOW ATTACKING CLEAR

RACKET

NET 5' 1"

FIG. 13. Attacking and defensive clears.

the height of your clearing stroke. If you are in a dangerous position or off-balance, clear as high as you possibly can, with the maximum of wrist in the stroke. Throw your racket head at the shuttle. If you are in a position, but your opponent is out of position, then clear low to give him as little time as possible to recover. But remember "quick over" is liable to a "quick back" reply.

Height is the key to attack or defence in clearing. There is no doubt that the stroke is looked on primarily as a defensive one, but there are many times in a rally when you will be able to turn the tables, use it offensively and obtain the point.

With deep clearing, err on the side of the very high clear rather than on the low clear. If you are well back in court, you will have to be feeling very strong or you will have to be playing with a pretty fast shuttle actually to clear it out of court. Far better for the shuttle to fall a few inches beyond the base line than a foot short. The first type of error is much more easily corrected. It is also most desirable that the shuttle falls perpendicularly on to your opponent, and that can happen only if you clear high.

Avoid if possible clearing straight down the court. This is the easiest of these strokes for your opponent to deal with: the cross-court clear—and it must be high to make sure it is not intercepted—will prove much trickier.

The forehand overhead clear is such an easy stroke to make providing you time it correctly that I think most beginners find the backhand difficult more by comparison than anything else. It is, of course, both the different footwork and the timing involved that complicate the execution of backhand strokes for most players.

This is a stroke you will find it difficult to master in the early stages. The problem is more easily solved if we know what the difficulties are and why they exist. When you have to take this shot from somewhere near the baseline, you will need a stroke of considerable power. This power is not easy to produce for two reasons. Firstly, in many cases you can hardly use the weight of your body at all. Secondly, the power must therefore come from the wrist and arm and will only be produced by exact and precise timing. This timing, to add to your difficulty, is less easy to produce on the backhand because to do it you may have to turn your back partly toward the shuttle.

Now we see the difficulties involved we can set about finding the solution to the problem. This lies in two stages. First, we accentuate the backhand position of the right foot well across the front of the body towards the left hand line. This will eliminate the body to a certain extent, and will allow you to get your arm well *across* the body and therefore well behind and below the shuttle.

The second stage is the timing. To help you with this, imagine your elbow is hinged, just like the hinge on a trunk. Point your elbow at the shuttle. Now when you judge the shuttle to be the right distance, shoot out your arm, unhinging it at the elbow joint. You should strike the shuttle with the arm straight again; and the wrist flick put in at the last moment will make it into a true power stroke.

This stroke needs practice. It would not be honest to lead you to think otherwise. At first you will make wood shots. Do not worry about that. Once you are hitting it, the fine adjustment can follow. The stroke is best practised by asking a fellow member in your club to throw up the shuttle as high as possible on to your backhand—as high as possible because that is the easiest position from which to take it.

As an aid to judging the height, try this experiment. Stand just inside a doorway in your house and point your right foot along the wainscot. Press your right leg against the doorpost, put your right arm above your head and slowly work it from the elbow with the hinge action, straight up the door post. If you are of average height you will reach over the top of the door post—and this is without a racket in your hand! From this you will see that a high clear on the backhand, taken at a fairly easy position, would be 8-9 feet off the ground.

If you are not too heavy a person, you may find it a help to raise yourself on to your right toe for this important stroke, either with or without keeping ground contact with the left foot, but preferably keeping contact. A certain amount of extra power is put into the stroke in this way.

On the other hand, you may find it easier to adopt the method of backhand clearing already touched on in the previous chapter under the heading "Footwork". This is to take the clear off the left foot (which is to the rear), hitting behind and upwards at the shuttle from a position where, if you let the shuttle fall, it would drop on your head or shoulder, or just behind. For this stroke you need to use the thumb-up grip. Your weight will remain on your left foot; it is not in this case transferred to your right foot, unless you decide to convert it into a drive stroke.

For all clearing strokes, aim at the ideal of a straight arm at impact. The importance of this becomes apparent if you watch a player's arm when he strikes the shuttle with this straightened arm. The wrist comes over automatically and immediately. If you wish to try it yourself, throw a ball and watch your own wrist flick over and downwards. If you hit *under* the shuttle, your wrist will flick over and force the shuttle upwards for a good clear.

The Smash

The Smash is the main attacking shot in badminton. It is a power stroke consisting of all sources of power unleashed on the shuttle when it is above *and in front of* the striker's head. The object is to send the shuttle on the fastest possible downwards path. A steep smash is a good one: a flat trajectory smash is a bad one.

To those readers who have played lawn tennis, the preliminaries of the Smash come easily. They are similar to those for a tennis overhead service or smash. To those who are new to both games, the usual stance is again sideways on to the net, with the body bent slightly backwards; this will help you to throw it into the shot at the right moment. For with the smash, timing is everything. If you are not supple enough or the wrong build anyway for this backward flexing from the waist, do not worry. Perfectly good smashes can be made by even corpulent players.

We have already tried the overhead clear. The preparations for the smash should look the same to your opponent. He must not know until the last moment, when the shuttle leaves your racket, which it is going to be. But the shuttle will not be struck for the smash until your body has begun its forward movement.

The exact position at which it should be struck varies slightly with the individual. This is so even with the experts.

A close study of the leading players over the past twenty-five years leads me to the conclusion that the *best* point is—as I mentioned in the opening paragraph of this section—above but just in front of the head. On the other hand, some of the best smashes I remember seeing —Ian Maconachie's and Bill White's for example*— appeared to be taken immediately above the head. If they had let the shuttle drop without hitting it, it would, I fancy, have perched on their shoulders. The leading Malayans I have seen, on the other hand, all hit their smashes well in front of their bodies: if they had let fall the shuttle, I think it would have dropped a foot in front of them. You must experiment a little here to find your ideal position. What is quite certain is that you must go *up and forward* to meet the shuttle. Left too late you will be falling over backwards when you hit it and you will produce that doleful stroke, a flat-trajectory smash which floats away beyond your opponent's baseline.

As you swing back, then, your weight will be on your right leg, your body flexed backwards from the waist. As you swing upwards and forward, your arm will straighten out, and strike the shuttle at its full extent. The last moment snap will come from the releasing of your cocked wrist. This becomes automatic (as we have already noted) if your arm has been straightened suddenly.

As you make contact with the shuttle, you will try to direct it on as steep a course as possible downwards into

* Famous international players of the nineteen 'thirties.

your opponents' court. You will bear in mind, when placing it, your opponents' likes and dislikes in this respect. This aspect of the smash will be examined in the chapter on tactics which follows later in this book.

The preparation and execution of the smash just described presumes you have had time to get ready for your stroke. Unfortunately, your opponent will seldom let you have this precious element, Time. You, for your part, will try to make time, but again this is not always possible. You must therefore cultivate a number of smashes taken from various positions, some good, some bad, some convenient, some very awkward.

The best way to get variety into your smash is to culti-vate the round-the-head smash, the most valuable of the variations. The first great player to cultivate this stroke was, I believe, Guy Sautter, three times All-England champion in the years before World War I, and later H. S. Uber. I never saw these players on court, but from all accounts H. S. Uber could lean right over to the left, taking the shuttle as low as head high and smashing it back on to his opponent's backhand. Later, some Canadian players—Don Smythe comes to mind—and the leading Danes demonstrated their prowess with the stroke, though none with particular severity.

It is an especially valuable stroke when dealing with a serve angled into your backhand from the right-hand court. Indeed it is the only really effective reply to this. The alternatives, taking the shuttle low on the backhand with an underarm clearing stroke, or executing a back-hand drop, both lay you open to swift retribution unless you are very careful.

The shot does require a certain suppleness at the waist, but remember that in the case of the angled service, once the shuttle has left your opponent's racket, you are allowed to vacate your service court and can move across the court to get under the shuttle. For many years I was leaning over into my partner's side of the court to reach these shots, as if there was a "Keep Off The Grass" notice on the other side of the centre line.

A smash can be hit off the wrong foot as well, when necessary. But this is far from ideal and only serves to emphasise that the shot must have that last minute wrist snap. A smash can also be hit from mid-air. It was Eddy Choong who made this stroke the hallmark of his game. But as he confessed to me once: "People expect me to do a few of those—and it does gain me height, although I know it's not strictly correct, nor always necessary."

He is quite right. But you must remember that Choong in his prime was a bundle of court quicksilver, light, wiry and as fit as a fiddle. The average club player of normal weight would soon find that this sort of smashing took too much out of him. People will not expect it of *you*. My advice is to stick to the orthodox smashes and keep your tendons intact. In any case, if you jump, your racket jumps too—and this serves only to increase the margin of error.

There are three distinct variations of the round-the-head smash. It can be taken as a forehand smash but leaning sideways to get in position under the shuttle and in this case your weight is first on the right foot (to the rear) and can then be transferred to the left if necessary. Or it can be taken facing the left hand side of the court, off the left foot (to the rear) with no transfer of weight. Or it can be taken sometimes off the right foot (to the front), providing that, as you receive it, it is not angled too deeply into the backhand corner of your service court.

These round-the-head smashes provide us with the exception to the rule about hitting your strokes with a straight arm at impact. In most cases, these have to be struck with a bent arm.

If you find this round-the-head smashing comes to you easily, you are lucky. It will add enormously to the attacking side of your game. But a word of caution. Do not take shots round the head which should by rights be backhand clears. It is an easy habit to fall into: there was even a semi-finalist overseas All-England player who had done this. He lost his key match after an otherwise expert performance. I blamed that flaw in his game. Too often it left him slightly out of position or off balance. There is a strong tendency for the stroke to force your body in the direction of the left side line.

There remains the backhand smash. I have heard players deny such a stroke exists. It if does, it lacks certainly the power of a forehand smash: Sir George Thomas described it as "a colourless imitation" of it. It has its uses, however, when played from somewhere near the net. It can be played cross court from even further back: John Best, the Kent and England player, made this difficult stroke look easy and Peter Waddell (Kent) cultivated it to great effect. When you are becoming expert, try to add it to your arsenal of badminton weapons. As a beginner, bear it in mind but do not feel your game lacks a lot because you have not mastered it yet. Your arm and wrist will provide almost all the power for the stroke. Until you have this developed you will produce nothing more than a fast backhand drop.

Remember that the pace of a smash is sometimes important: but the *placing* of a smash is always important. The steep smash to an unoccupied part of the court is an obvious winner. But in doubles it is often the slightly higher smash across a player's body which will earn the point. This calls for more movement of the racket, giving less time to swing the racket at the shuttle, either with the wrist or the arm and wrist.

The steep smash I have mentioned should go no further

Upper Left:
THE COCKED WRIST (HEATHER WARD)

Upper Right:
HIGH FOREHAND DROP (HEATHER WARD)

Below:
LOW FOREHAND DROP (HEATHER WARD)
taken two strides from centre line

THE BACKHAND CLEAR

PREPARATION

SHORTLY BEFORE IMPACT

than mid-court. When you are learning to smash, aim
first at the tape. Do not worry if your shots plough into
the net. As you practise, raise your smash a little until
you are hitting the tape. Then raise it again a degree
until your shuttles are clearing the tape. It is much
easier to do it this way than to practise flat smashing to
the baseline and beyond, a bad habit easily formed but
difficult to break.

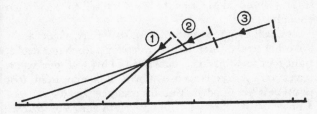

Fig. 14. The angles of the smash. (1) Steep angle smash (good),
(2) Mid-court smash (sometimes good), (3) Shallow smash to baseline (least effective).

The Drop

We will deal with the Drop shot now for this reason.
The Clear is the most commonly used stroke in the game.
The Smash is a point winner. But combine good drop
shots with accurate clears and you have a basis for sound
badminton in any language.

The essence of a drop, which can be played from any
position and from any part of the court, is the steepness
of its fall near the net. Because all drop shots are slow
shots, they must be accurate. To keep them accurate
means especial care in stroking. The shuttle must be hit
gently but firmly. It needs little punch, but the maximum
guidance.

But before we proceed with the mechanics of making a

drop shot, a word of warning. Please resist the temptation to use the drop shot too often. It is by far the most fascinating of all the strokes, and the most satisfying except for an actual "kill". But therein lies the danger. Too many drops are made in badminton when the shuttle should have been hit down for a winner. A prominent international of the nineteen-fifties—who shall be nameless—nearly lost his place in the English team, I fancy, because of over-addiction to the drop shot. He had a beautiful smash—but couldn't seem to bring himself to use it often enough.

You will use the same foot position for drop shots as for the other strokes—left foot forward for a forehand stroke, right foot forward for a backhand. This will give you a reasonably well balanced platform. You may think foot position is less important in this instance because it is not a power stroke. But you will do well to cultivate the correct position of the feet even for these shots, because you will need to deceive your opponent whenever possible. You do this by occasionally not playing a drop at all—when it is expected—but by suddenly changing your stroke to a power shot—when you need your feet correctly placed.

Indeed, for overhead strokes, your drop shot will often be executed to best effect when your opponent is expecting a power stroke, a smash or a full length clear. Using these foot positions then, you will meet the shuttle as early as possible. Let us take the overhead drop from mid-court first. You will more often than not smash this; but if your opponents are both towards the back of the court, one perhaps off balance, the other in a poor position, the smash will be substituted by a drop shot. With the same preliminary movements you will begin the motions for a clear but at the last moment you will slow the arm down and reduce the amount of flexing of your arm and wrist, so striking the shuttle comparatively gently. This will cause it to drop down sharply, taking a downwards course all the way from your racket to the far side of the net, only just clearing the net cord and falling thereafter very steeply. (See diagram.)

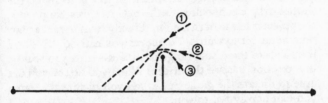

Fig. 15. Drop shot trajectories. (1) Steep angle drop, (2) Mid-court drop with "travel", (3) Net drop (or Coconut drop).

These overhead drops can be made from any part of the court and from various angles. Accuracy is less easy on the backhand, but the backhand cross court drop is a winner worth cultivating. Remember the idea is that it drops steeply as soon as it has crossed the net. And you must make sure the particular side of the net at which you are aiming is not in possession of an opposing net player.

The same class of drop can be executed with underarm strokes, but has a strong element of danger about it. This is because in the former case the shuttle was travelling downwards along its whole path. Stroked underarm, the shuttle will be travelling upwards for a large part of its journey. It will require very fine judgment, almost perfection, to arrange its flight path so that it drops as soon as it has crossed the net. And if it doesn't, then your opponent will make short work of it.

The farther you get back in court, the more difficult the judging of the drop shot will become. Because of this, you should use the drop shot much less from the back of the court, more often from the front of the court when your steeply dropping shuttle will have your opponents stretched along the floor scraping the shuttle up—for you to put down.

There is another type of drop shot. In the instances we have been considering, the prime object is to make the shuttle drop steeply close to the net. In this second class, the object is less to earn a point directly than to make your opponents hit upwards. Whenever you can do this—and it applies to the whole range of strokes—then you will be in a position to seize the attack. When you attack you are able to dictate the game and when you dictate the game you can hardly fail to win.

This slightly faster type of drop is quite useful when you yourself are not too close to the net, but your opponents include a fast net lady. Played in this circumstance, your drop shot, overhead or underarm, will clear the net a few inches above it but dropping several feet beyond it, possibly beyond the reach of the lady, but causing her partner to scoop up the shuttle rather late and hit it upwards ready for you to attack.

Until quite recent years, any slicing movement at badminton has been frowned on in most circumstances. But the best Asians playing over here have had such success with it that it has become much more widely used. The danger of a slicing action is that you may produce a mis-hit. The advantages are that since the wrist and racket are turned sideways at point of impact, the pace is taken right out of the stroke and it falls rapidly at a steep angle. Some prefer to call these strokes half-angle smashes, mainly because they begin as a smash but are converted into something approaching an angled drop shot at the last moment. I have seen players new to this completely baffled at this stroke in singles play; and found it baffling myself when Malayans first used it against me in practice play, in spite of being well prepared for it and receiving verbal warning before the "execution"!

Lady net players' reputations will rest almost entirely on a good short service and the quality of their delicate drop shots. These strokes do not *look* all that impressive— but how important they are! They provide the opening from which the man will seize his chance to smash. It is particularly important when playing drop shots at the net to take the shuttle very early, as high as possible. There are a number of good reasons for this. In the first place, the longer you leave it, the more time your opponent has to get into position for the next stroke. Secondly, the more difficult it will be for you to make an effective stroke (indeed, if it is near the floor when you reach it, you have no alternative but to hit well upwards and hope for the best). Thirdly, the sooner you turn it back over the net, the less margin you leave for your own error. Taken a mere inch or two from the top of the net, the shuttle will literally bounce itself back over the net, with a minimum of assistance from you. Better still take the shuttle as it crosses the tape, tapping it smartly down to win the point there and then.

The only exception to this rule of taking the shuttle as early as possible is when the shuttle has toppled over the net, which is commonly called a net-cord. Before you can hit this cleanly or accurately you will have to let it regain its natural flight characteristic of base first. Keep calm in these circumstances, avoiding any suspicion of panic. Avoid, too, being mesmerised by this unusual (?) occurrence. Wait a second or two to decide what the shuttle is up to, then play on.

It is interesting to note in this connection that the originators of badminton never saw fit to have the net reach the ground, as with lawn tennis for example. The inference is that, at somewhere near ground level, the shuttle may be struck—to execute a cross court drop for instance—and the racket head follow through under the net into your opponents' court. As with the shuttle struck close to the net cord, the rules do not make this stroke illegal.

The Drive

The Drive is probably the least-used of the basic badminton strokes. The reason for this is the ease of interception, especially in doubles. It is simply a flat stroke aimed to skim the net, travelling on a course roughly in a line parallel to the floor. It is normally hit at a point lower than chest level—otherwise you would try to take it overhead—but from the back of the court can be hit from a point right down to knee level. From this level, it ceases to be an attacking stroke and becomes a stroke of despair, its only advantage over a clearing stroke being that it gives your opponents much less time should they be out of position.

It is taught in some quarters that the drive can vary in pace, but I prefer to think always of a drive as a hard hit shot, preferably an attacking stroke. If you soft-pedal on it, stroke it gently, then it is nothing more than a drop shot taken with a sideways sweep of the racket.

Try to take the drive as early as possible, not too low and ensure again that you put plenty of wrist into the final action. Tactically, the cross-court drive should be used only rarely. Down-the-line drives are much safer, as you will see when we examine simple tactics.

The forehand whipped drive can be taken off the right foot and should actually be *aimed* at the tape. It should be directed cross court only if a direct winner can be seen. The reason for this is that it takes longer to travel.

There is one further use for a drive. That is to return a

smash. It was Mrs. Uber, I think, who was the last top
flight player to use this regularly and effectively. It
requires quite a lot of practice and a sound sense of
timing. But off all but the steepest smashes she was able
to drive the shuttle back into her opponents' court,
using much of their speed. It was a most effective way of
turning an attacking stroke against the opponents and
regaining the defence with one swift countermove.

I have left this drive stroke to the last because I consider it the least important for a beginner. When you are
teaching yourself it is important to build up your game
step by step. It is especially important that you gain
confidence as you go along. If you can serve well, clear
and drop, you will already be welcomed as a partner. The
Smash will come along automatically once you are
clearing well overhead and it is unwise to hurry it in the
early stages because of its essential element of timing. In
the same way, you can play good badminton, especially
the singles game, with very little driving. Leave it to the
last and tack it on your game when you feel you have
mastered the other basic strokes. There are certain times
in doubles when it is invaluable: but you will need to
know something about the tactical side of the game
before you can spot these occasions. In the two chapters
following we will examine simple tactics: the more
complicated strategies will be left to you to work out in
your later badminton life.

Net Strokes

Before I leave the actual matter of stroke-making I
would like to draw your attention to the several odd and
varied strokes the ladies make at the net, particularly in
mixed doubles. These are all important strokes but are
built up on the others and are sometimes difficult to
define. With the thumb-up grip we have mentioned, the

ladies can tap down the shuttle in an uncannily accurate manner. They add to these telling net interceptions such shots as the Stab, the Rush, the Dab and the Push Shot—names which are practically self-explanatory. With the exception, sometimes, of the last-named, these are all clever attacking strokes, in spite of the soppy names we have given them.

There is an amusing story about the Push Shot, recounted by Mrs. Uber in her book "That Badminton Racket". It recalls the peculiar, shuffling low service of Miss H. Hogarth (an English international from 1905-1924). After executing it she would crouch down to enable her partner to see the shuttle. Mrs. Uber's husband (also an international player) would pretend to rush these low services, but as soon as Miss Hogarth had crouched would alter his shot and just push the shuttle gently on to her back, often winning 8 or 9 points in a match in this manner. "Although Miss Hogarth was the first to see the humour of it and appreciate a good shot," Mrs. Uber writes, "the look she gave him as she shook the shuttle off her back spoke volumes."

CHAPTER VIII

SIMPLE SINGLES TACTICS

Do not be put off by the word tactics. By dictionary definition, it comprises simply the use of a procedure calculated to gain some end—in this case the winning of a game of badminton. Above all, do not fall for that line: "The more I think about it, the worse I get"—a purely defeatist attitude.

As with lawn tennis, there are certain "types" of badminton player, and most of us will conform to one of them. To some extent this will govern the tactics we shall use normally. That is to say, an aggressive type of player will base his game, quite naturally, on the smash and the drive. The quieter, touch player, will use more drops, clears and half-angle smashes. Again, the aggressive type will rarely have the patience to play a waiting game, while the quieter type will gain many points this way, trading profitably on his opponent's errors.

And there, of course, is the rub. Your opponent. For he, too, will have a considerable say in what sort of game you play—your tactics. If he is much stronger than you, you will need to play a defensive game anyway. Contrariwise, if he is normally not an aggressive player, but finds himself stronger than you, he may be forced to adopt something in the nature of an attacking game—and in not playing the game he prefers to play, fall into a crop of errors.

You will find then in practice that you have certain natural tactical inclinations. The thing you must aim to do is to know when to abandon them and to be able to play a different tactical game. When I say "when to abandon them", you must appreciate that the tactics of play will change several times during a game, due to such factors as the state of the game, your condition and your opponent's condition and the effect your play is having—both on you and him.

In badminton there is a clear distinction between the two main categories of tactical play: in a nut-shell, defensive play is when you are hitting the shuttle upwards, attacking play when you are hitting it downwards. Since when you are hitting up the shuttle is falling for a longer period of time, this is slowing down the game. When you are constantly hitting down, the pace of the game is increased.

Clearly, an attacking game is best. But badminton is such a strenuous game, especially in singles, that constant smashing against a cast-iron defence is a certain way to burn yourself out and fall an easy prey to your opponent's *defensive* game.

Before you begin to find this complicated, let's split the tactical problem in two: singles and doubles.

(I would like to digress for a moment at this point to explain why I shall bring the name and game of Eddy Choong into this chapter. You may think I have said enough about him previously. In the first place it is difficult to separate singles tactics from personalities—it is very much a personal matter. Secondly, as the leading singles player in England during my own playing "life" in club badminton, I had the opportunity of studying many of his matches. And, finally, on his return to Malaya after 6 years in London, he left me a number of unedited notes on the game with permission to use them where and when I liked.)

Singles

The basic idea in singles is to move your opponent

around the court as much as possible, and to move him away from his base position. You will eventually force him to put up a weak shot which you can hit down. You will move him round by alternating drops and clears, clearing whenever possible deep to his backhand corner.

The way to begin this process is with a high service, as deep as possible so that it falls perpendicularly. This is more difficult for him to smash and usually elicits the reply of a clear.

To continue with an actual stroke sequence, assume you now have his clear to deal with. If this has been struck deep, he will be somewhere at the back of the court. You will offer a drop shot to the left hand side of the net, which he will have to run in to take. He will probably make the safest reply, a further clearing stroke off his forehand to your backhand corner. You now clear this with an over-head clear from somewhere near your backhand corner to his backhand corner. This causes him the maximum amount of running—backwards. His reply to this should be the weak one which you will hit down to win the point.

As a rule of thumb, you will try to use the four corners of the half-court, avoiding all the time the centre, pivot position. No shuttle should be directed to this part of the court, which he will use as base. (See diagram) Fig. 16.

Eddy Choong had a slightly different angle on this, perfectly valid. He aimed first to move his opponent into the backhand corner with a clearance stroke to this part of the court, then to attack him there by continuing to place the shuttle there. From this you will see that a pre-requisite of either tactic is that you must have the stroke with which to do it. You need to be able to clear to his backhand corner from anywhere in your half of the court.

Here it should be noted that when I refer to clear, I do

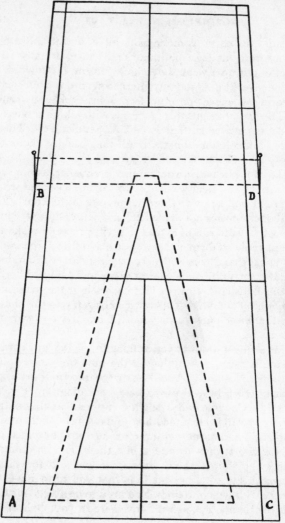

FIG. 16. The pivot position. Based in the triangles, you can reach easily points A, B, C, and D.

not necessarily mean a *high* clear. Indeed, if your opponent is the type of player who has an effective counterstroke given time for preparation, you will not allow him this. You will not allow him the time by low clearing to his backhand corner. He may reach it because of its low trajectory, but will often then mis-hit it.

Singles play at badminton has something in common with noughts and crosses. By making a certain stroke you can force a known reply. And forewarned is forearmed. Knowing where that reply is likely to be, you will be in position to deal with it drastically.

These remarks apply to men's single. Ladies' singles (only to 11 points, not 15 as with men's) are similar, but differ to some extent because the speed of the players is usually slower and their stamina rather less than that of men players. Because of this, the smash is less favoured, and most of the play is based on variations of drop and clear.

There are certain strokes which are less effective in singles because you have no partner: and there are others which are more effective than in doubles.

Among the more effective strokes I class the stroke so seldom used by club players, the half-smash—as it used to be called—or the half-angle smash, as the Malayans usually call it. Too many players come to think of a smash as hitting the shuttle as hard as possible in a downward direction. This is a kill. But a smash can be just as effective—and more so in many circumstances—if it is *not* hit with full force. A full force stroke may take the shuttle back right on to your opponent's racket. Hit with a sideways stroking action, it will drop more sharply, probably at an angle, on the later part of its flight and cause him to run towards it complying again with our basic idea of moving your opponent around. These half smashes can be stroked off in either direction, without

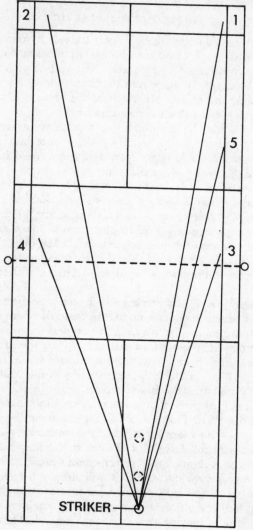

FIG. 17. Singles tactics. The striker can make
the 5 returns indicated.

your opponent knowing which side it will come, or, indeed, if it will not be after all a full power smash.

In any case, avoid stereotyping your tactical play. Club players are most prone to this grooving of their play, probably because the scores are not recorded and are of little account. Many have one game only and are predictable for every stroke. For this reason, a player a class above them seizes the tactical advantage almost in the opening rally. As soon as you have mastered the basic strokes, inject variety and deception into your play and you will have laid the basis of a sound tactical game.

When I was preparing this book, I asked that fine Malayan player Oon Chong Teik, nephew of the famous Wong Peng Soon, if he thought Eddy Choong was right to play his fabulous games against Joe Alston of America and Finn Kobbero of Denmark defensively. He thought he *was* right, for, by comparison (he thought) Choong was a player at that time—1956-57—without many strokes but with terrific stamina and courtcraft.

"In these matches," Oon said, "Choong's main strokes were his lob and his drop, both perfected. These two strokes are really the essential in badminton. Eddy will always defeat such opponents not because he is superior all round but because he can run them to a standstill and outwit them. He seldom risked net play, but flicked the shuttle away to the back of the court. He only risked a net shot when his opponent was elsewhere in court. Choong's smash is far from lethal, too. It's his deception there that gains him points."

In an effort to find out more about these star players' tactics, I also questioned Oon about Kobbero. This is what he thought of "the Great Dane" in 1958.

"The trouble with Finn is that he has brilliant shots combined with terrible ones. He lacks concentration. He always tries to score a point with one stroke. When he has a good spell, he is untouchable—with a terrific backhand drop, strong smash and good net play. To attack Finn is not easy: a defensive waiting game is better against him."

And Alston?

"He is a player with good stamina, a smash and moderate strokes. He also has a very deceptive drop shot. The reason Eddy and Joe's matches went on for so long (they once played a first game of 18-16 for over an hour) is that both were fit and were trying to outlast each other."

You won't play Alston or Choong at singles. They retired from this branch of the game in the 1957-58 season. But Oon and Kobbero and Choong will be about for a few years yet, I imagine. I hope the foregoing will help you to plan your singles tactics against them! You must think about your opponents as Oon thinks about his opponents. This "thinking around" is important in order to develop your own tactics.

I began by saying that you should try to move your opponent around the court, to get him away from his base position in the centre of the court. By the same token, you must strive to retain your base position. When out of this position you will often play a slow shot (a clear or a slow mid-court drop) in order to regain your base. It is height which will gain you time. There are two planes to consider. In the horizontal plane you will direct your shots and try to anticipate the replies almost by geometry. But you must also keep in mind the vertical plane: and this always involves the time factor.

Alston himself is a great believer in the mental attitude. He assumes that any outstanding player will have all the basic shots and wide experience. Then why can't this player win? "He must be completely convinced in his own mind that he is the best player," Alston says, "that he is capable of beating anyone at any time. He must feel sure he is in equal or better physical condition than his opponent: that he can return any shots his opponent hits: and that his opponent will crack before he will."

This is, of course, unvarnished, the "killer" philosophy, not beloved of British sportsmen or sportswomen. It is said to help you play better when things are going against you. Dave Freeman, probably the best badminton player of all time, gave Alston an alternative solution to the problem by stating "if you get behind or things are not going too well, slow the game down to a walk in your own mind."

This much is certain. If you aspire to singles honours, you must develop *some* positive mental attitude toward your matches: and you must develop a sense of timing at least as good as a first-rate actor's sense of timing.

CHAPTER IX

SIMPLE DOUBLES TACTICS
(Mixed—Men's—Ladies)

Doubles

The most important thing in doubles is your partner.
Your tactics will be based on a realistic assessment of
each other's capabilities. There is a fundamental difference between singles and doubles. In doubles you can get
away with shots played to the wrong place, you can even
get away with shots played at quite the wrong time—
providing you are not giving your opponents the time to
do anything about it.

This *rapport* between partners is a basic part of doubles.
Two brilliant players do not make, necessarily, a good
pair. It is complementary talents that yield the finest
partnerships. You have doubtless seen the partnerships
that fail on the court. The player who denigrates his
partner in front of the opposition because he missed a
"sitter". When I see this I am always reminded of golf
writer Bernard Darwin's: "It is not a crime to play a bad
shot and the player may yet be a good husband and
father and a true Christian gentleman."

After combination, I would place a good serve as the
next most important requirement for doubles. The
service must be varied, but, generally speaking, this means
a good, low serve. The idea here is that, from the
opening stroke, you are inviting your opponent to hit
up—so that you or your partner can hit down. This is
particularly important in mixed doubles. There has been

no really successful post-war mixed partnership that did not include an accurate low service.

The next important tactical point is Time. You need to be ahead of your opponents, gaining time, so that you deny them this precious badminton commodity. If you get into position for a stroke early enough, you not only have the chance to execute it as you wish, but you also have the time to choose which stroke you will make. This time for choice leaves your opponents with a corresponding period of doubt. In men's doubles, the speed of the game sometimes invalidates this, but it is particularly applicable in mixed doubles in the front-and-back formation.

When presented with a choice of strokes, choose whenever possible the one you can hit down. This not only conforms to our basic principle but also allows your opponents less time. The exception to this is when you (or your partner) are out of position and you wish to have time to regain these lost positions.

Another problem will crop up in doubles. It is that of body-elimination. If the shuttle is directed straight at your body, you must try to pivot on your right or left foot and bring the other foot back sharply. This will enable you to get your racket to the shuttle and make a defensive reply. You will find it easier in many cases to pivot on the right foot and take the shot on the backhand.

It is necessary when considering badminton doubles to sub-divide. There are men's and women's doubles and there is mixed doubles, a game requiring a different tactical approach entirely. Again, there are three distinct doubles formations in popular use, the back-and-front— by far the most common for mixed—the side-by-side formation; and a third which is, in effect, a combination of the two.

Mixed Doubles

Since mixed doubles is the most popular form of the game, I shall give it pride of place. It is wise to appreciate straight away that, in normal combinations, the man, playing at the back of the court, will be the more active member of the pair, the lady playing at the net, a less spectacular but none the less vital role. This leads us to a division of labour. The lady should be content to serve low and accurately—to force the receivers to hit up—to counter drop shot with drop shot and to deal drastically with any loose shot that comes her way. The man should smash whenever possible and take all the shots that pass his partner.

Here lies the rub of the doubles problem. As a man, the ideal partner is the lady who knows, almost instinctively, what shots you are able and willing to take, and what shots you will expect her to intercept. This fine judgment comes only with experience. It is the main reason why scratch partnerships in tournaments nearly always fail.

This is also the reason why really good mixed pairs in back-and-front formation are seldom seen in ordinary club play (outside the club teams). After sitting out in the cold waiting for her turn to play, a lady can hardly be expected to crouch under the net while her partner has a nice warming game! I recommend side-by-side formation in these circumstances.

There is little doubt, nonetheless, that the back-and-front is the best mixed doubles formation in at least 9 cases out of 10. It is so because it confines each part of the game to the player with the right capabilities. The feminine touch can work miracles of *finesse* at the net. Few men can compare. But not one woman in a hundred "plays like a man" (and who would wish her to do so). The man's role is the attacking strokes, the smashes and the power drives down the line. Even should a woman

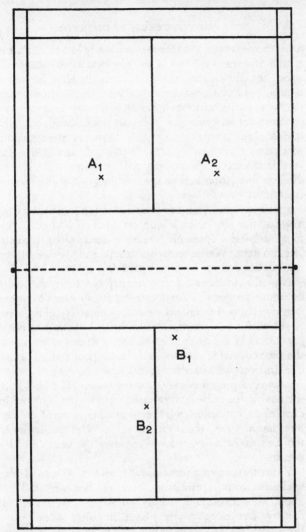

FIG. 18. A1 and A2, playing side-by-side are in a defensive formation. B1 and B2, playing up-and-back, are in an attacking formation.

have these strokes, her stamina is usually less than that of a man and she would soon become exhausted.

But in all doubles tactics, and particularly in mixed tactics, what is sometimes called the Compensation Factor must be considered before you go on court for any serious play and must be borne in mind throughout the match. This is, quite simply; what is my strength and weakness, what is my partner's strength and weakness? In this summing up, modesty will get you nowhere. And the best formation will be the one that makes the most of your joint capabilities.

I will imagine you, the reader, for the moment as my new partner for a mixed doubles match this evening. Due to an influenza epidemic, we have been called in at the last moment. We have arrived early and we are discussing tactics before the others arrive.

Now for my personal assessment; as I have said, with no undue modesty. I have a strong smash when I can get it going, a good forehand clear and a variety of all types of serve. I am weak on the backhand clear, am not a great deal of use at the net and am rather vulnerable to the service angled into my backhand. (Look at my waistline and you will see why!) Now how about you?

Miss Smith is encouraged by my frankness. She admits she has played quite a bit of singles so is farly strong on the deep clear, can smash a bit, can take her place at the net, but "has a thing" about the low serve. "I'm usually much too nervous at the start to do any over the net at all" she admits.

From this we can work out our tactics. We shall play back-and-front formation, of course. But we shall not adopt this formation strictly speaking until after the first two strokes have been played in many of the rallies. For these reasons. I am vulnerable to the angled service into my backhand. Miss Smith will compensate for this by falling back a little when I serve, because my reply may be a weakish clear eliciting a hit down from my opponents.

Similarly, if Joy Smith has no low serve in her repertoire it's not much use her learning at our expense tonight. She will hit up an angled lob service over her opponent's head from mid-court and both of us will wait, with a fair amount of time, for the return.

In both these cases, we shall adopt the back-and-front formation as soon as possible afterwards. We shall not remain side by side longer than necessary, however, because if we did I could not bring into play my smash often enough, nor could she show her mettle at the net. I think the male member of these partnerships in this formation must bear in mind that it is unfair to ask a lady to play at the net for him, to make his opponents hit up, unless he can produce the necessary winner off the opening she has made. So in this form of mixed doubles, a man must eschew all drop shots (except the occasional one for deceptive purposes) and hit down hard at every opportunity. Compensating for this, the lady should not try to produce winners by smashing or driving, but should concentrate on drop or push shots to elicit these hit up returns from the other side of the net. The watchword for the lady will be Restraint, for the man Attack.

Now this is the little tactical exercise we have indulged in, Miss Smith and I, *before* we have met our opponents. As in singles tactics, what goes on the other side of the net can often upset our applecart.

You have probably assumed—and in most cases you would be quite right—that your opponents will be playing a back-and-front formation. As soon as you begin to knock up you will note any apparent weaknesses, where and in which one of the pair lies the apparent strength, and adjust your plans accordingly.

But supposing the formation facing you is a side-by-side pair? This pre-supposes two good hitters, two players not quite so happy at the net. Accordingly, you will play a larger percentage of drop shots than you would have done otherwise, and where you must clear you will clear high and deep.

You think the sides system looks simpler to operate? Theoretically, I suppose it is. On court it does not seem to work any simpler. Basically, you merely divide the court into two down the middle and agree that anything on your half of the court you take, anything on the other is your partner's. Simple, isn't it! But is it so simple? Firstly, who is playing on the left, who on the right? You have to bear in mind that the player on the left will get a higher percentage of shots to take from the backhand corner. Who takes a drop shot at the centre of the net? If you serve low and the return is a drop shot to the opposite side of the court, will you follow your low serve in and take it? You will then be forced into a back-and-front formation, won't you? No, rigid adherence to a side-by-side formation is far from easy in mixed doubles, a little less difficult in men's, where partners are of the same relative strength.

There is the third formation left for us to consider, the one which is a mixture of the two we have already dealt with. This is called In-and-Out by the Malayans, Rotational by the Americans—and all manner of names by those who cannot make it work!

The system involves the players circling, usually anti-clockwise. If the player on the right of the court advances to the net, the player on the left automatically drops back, and, as and when the player at the net cross to the left at the net, crosses to the right at the back of the court. This can be played in mixed doubles, but requires a great deal of liaison and practise with the same partner.

It is most suitable for ladies' doubles and it will be considered further under that heading.

To sum up. For mixed doubles, choose to play back-and-front formation where possible and keep in mind that the prime object is to attack, the man by hitting down from the back of the court, his partner by hitting down from the front of the court. The lady should go into the net to attack there, the division of the court being roughly one third for the lady, two thirds for the man.

In the back-and-front formation (sometimes called up-and-back) a typical opening to a rally, lady serving to lady, would be this. The lady server (A) serves low to receiving lady (B). B drops low across the net to the opposite side of the court to A's service court. But A gets to the shot, although with no alternative but to clear to the base line. This clear is of poor length, falls short, and is smashed by B's partner, C. A's partner D has, however, anticipated the smash well and gets his racket to it. His forced reply, a mid-court drop, is nevertheless intercepted by B, who pushes the shuttle down steeply into an unoccupied part of the opponent's court. A reaches the shuttle again and with a fast, mid-court drop wins the point, so serves again.

To add variety to her serving, and because the receiving man, C, is standing very close in, A pops her next serve over his head. C goes back quickly and smashes. But he is hurried, so smashes rather wildly and not too well towards the server A who has moved in to the net. A again taps the shuttle down to win the point. (The smash should have been down the line away from the net lady: or a high clear would have restored the position.)

Men's Doubles

Men's doubles is a very different form of the game from mixed and so a different set of considerations applies when we come to tactics. The reason for this lies mainly in the greater speed at which the game is played; the greater number of smashes and power strokes employed; and the more even sharing of both the court and the play.

This even sharing of the court and play is the basis of any good partnership. In many cases it extends to playing *for* your partner, that is to say making the openings for him to play his best shot and therefore win the rally. If he is striving to do the same for you, you can well imagine the stream of winners which will come off your rackets.

After teamwork, I would say the next most important requirements of men's doubles play is severity. Except in the very top class, there is always too much clearing. A clearing stroke will rarely win you the rally and passes the attack on a plate to your opponents. In singles, the deep clear to the base line is a sound move: in doubles I think it should be avoided unless specifically to drive one of your opponents back or to give you time to regain your own position in court. The low clear is better tactically. On the other hand, no harm can come to you at all if you make your high clear really high and deep: there is nothing damaging which your opponents can do with it.

The formation to adopt for men's doubles is side-by-side, or round-and-round (rotational). You are in the best defensive position when you are side-by-side—but do not base your game on defence. To clarify the round-and-round game, you may picture it better by the phrase in-and-out. You will occasionally run in to the net to take a drop shot (or your partner if he is better placed) after which you drop back into the half of the court which you vacated. But if you do move across the court, you move in a prearranged direction, usually anti-clockwise. Both you and your partner's movements will be governed by your opponents' positions in court.

Let's imagine for a minute that you have teamed up with a doubles partner and are going on court for your first match. We will assume you have mastered all the basic strokes and are of about equal standard of play.

You have won the toss and elected to serve (since both ends appear the same to you). You have chosen service because, with opponents who are new to you and no apparent advantage in end, you put yourself in the position of being able to score. Your chances are as good as their's in the opening rallies, because all players will be "cold" and feeling their way.

You want to attack, of course, but the rules (unlike lawn tennis) prevent you doing this with your first stroke. You take up your position, about a yard from the short service line and close to the centre line, and pause. During this pause, you take stock. You note where your opponent is standing; for if he is positioned other than in the same relative position in court as yourself, you will angle your shot to that part of the court he is not covering too well. You have three choices: a low serve, a lob serve or a drive.

The drive serve should be used rarely in men's doubles, but is effective as a surprise stroke. Angled into your opponent's backhand corner it can be most effective, but if he has a round-the-head smash you are wasting your time. The lob serve is also of little value in men's doubles unless it is really deep and is worked in on occasion to keep him from getting too near to the net and so being in a strong position to rush your short service. There is the flick lob service, of course, and this is really just as effective for ensuring he does not threaten the net too closely. This clears his height of 10 feet (with outstretched arm and racket) and sends him scuttling back, often without time to gather himself for an orthodox smash.

This leaves you with a low serve. This is the basis of all

good serving. No badminton player can afford to be without it. It is well worth every hour you spend practising it. This low serve should just skim the net cord *as it loses height*. Look at the two trajectory curves in the diagram below. A is right. B is wrong. A will force the receiver to hit it up, B will enable him to hit it down. So serve low to the centre line as the opening shot. But you will not be able to obtain the ideal trajectory if you stand in too close.

FIG. 19. A is a good low servive, B is a poor low service,
liable to be knocked down.

Now your opponent can do one of two things with this good service of yours. He can play a drop shot back to the centre of the court. You are well placed to counter this by taking the shuttle as high and as soon as it has crossed the net. He will then be forced to play the shuttle up into the air again, or to drop a second time. As he has just tried this without effect, it is likely that he will clear to get the shuttle away from you to some other part of the court.

The alternative will be to clear straight away off your low serve. This he will do over your head into the unoccupied corner of the court behind you. If you are playing strictly side-by-side formation, you will fall back and take the shuttle with a smash if in time, or an overhead clear if not. If you are playing in-and-out, you will move in and across the court, while your partner moves across the court behind you to take the shot. If he deep clears, then you will fall back to a mid-court position, ready for a smash off his clear. But if he half-angle smashes (or tries a drop shot) then you will remain closer to the net in readiness for your opponent's possible riposte of a drop shot.

Does this sound complicated? It will not, once you get playing. Badminton is not unlike chess. Sir George Thomas illustrated this lesson well, for he was a champion and an international at both games. You plan ahead in badminton. You do get a few opportunities to make outright winners, but many more rallies can be won by probing your opponents' weaknesses and then exploiting them.

So far in this section, we have been assuming you were the server. Cross the net a minute and try receiving. It is most important in men's doubles that you threaten the serve. Do not neglect this elementary principle. It has sound reasoning behind it. If you do not threaten the server, (1) he can settle down to produce his best shots.

(2) his weak serves will go unpunished.

(3) it will not enable you to seize the attack.

How do you threaten the server? You do this by assuming an aggressive stance, close in to the short service line, with racket raised behind your shoulder. (How close in, as I have pointed out elsewhere, depends on how quickly you can get back should he flick a serve over your head.) Having pounced on the serve, there is no going back! If it was a good serve, very low over the net, you will bend your knees and return the shuttle close to the net with a push shot, making the shuttle fall as steeply down the other side of the net as possible. This is the sort of drop the Malayans have nicknamed the Coconut drop. If the serve was not all that good, you will hit it downwards or straight back at the server's right shoulder. It is as well to have an understanding with your partner that when you do this he will cover the back of the court for the next stroke, leaving you to jump on any weak reply your own attacking stroke may have elicited. If your opponents get back a reasonable shot and the rally continues, then you will fall back into your side-by-side position and wait for another chance.

Ladies' Doubles

Many of the basic doubles principles which apply to men's and mixed doubles still apply to ladies' doubles. In a partnership where one lady is "as strong as a man" then you can apply them as you would for a mixed, the strong lady playing at the back of the court, her partner at the net. If both ladies are strong hitters, then they will adopt a similar formation to a men's doubles side-by-side or rotational formation. But in most cases, I suppose, the two ladies involved will be of about the same standard and neither very powerful hitters.

Ladies' doubles has been called the dullest form of the game. This criticism is only valid where neither lady has any attacking strokes. It must be admitted that in nine cases out of ten, a ladies' doubles defence is stronger than its attack. This arises because very few ladies can smash really hard but they are used to taking men's smashes in mixed doubles. When they come against the softer smashing of a ladies' doubles, they have no difficulty at all in coping with it. That it can be an exciting form of the game to watch has been shown by various county pairs' efforts to record wins against that amazingly successful pair of the 1950's, Mrs. June Timperley (née White) and Mrs. Iris Rogers (née Cooley).

The Timperley-Rogers formation is primarily an in-and-out one, but when possible, Mrs. Timperley in and Mrs. Rogers out, at the back of the court. The strongest pre-1939 combination of Mrs. Betty Uber and Diana Doveton was similar, for although Mrs. Uber was a brilliant singles player, a great number of their points came from Miss Doveton smashing from behind Mrs. Uber who waited at the net to finish off the rally with a beautifully-timed interception.

When you are beginning badminton, it is best to play a side-by-side game and then develop it into a rotational or in-and-out formation. When serving, you can freely mix short serves and lob serves: when receiving, you will smash all but the best high serves, clearing the others, while the low serves you will rush where possible, play into mid-court where you cannot.

As with all doubles, there are several points you will need to cover in the powder room before you go on court. These include: which of you will cover a short return of service, which will take drop shots to the centre of the net, which will go for centre-court smashes? You also need a clear understanding that whichever of you smashes, she will not be called on to cover the net for a possible return to that part of the court.

CHAPTER X

CORRECTING YOUR FAULTS—KEEPING FIT—OUTDOOR BADMINTON

IT has long puzzled me why nobody expects to play the piano or the violin without hours and hours of practice, yet is disappointed when he cannot execute strokes of a racket game that have taken a champion years to perfect. If you are what is called a natural, you probably won't need this book. But for the thousands who must learn the hard way, the first step in correcting your faults should be plenty of practice on the right lines so that you don't develop many faults anyway.

Yet there are a number of common ones which are bound to creep in however closely you have followed our instructions. These I have split up under five headings. They are:— Stroking Faults, Back Court Faults, Net Faults, Serving Faults, and Faults Receiving Service. Where possible, I have tried to indicate how you can correct them.

Stroking Faults.

1. Lack of wrist.   Correction: loosen grip on racket until actual moment of contact. Practise by imaginary "waving goodbye" with a perfectly limp wrist.

2. Ignoring sources of power.   Correction: bend knees slightly more when preparing to smash or high clear . . . loop racket further

THE SMASH

Upper Left:
PREPARATION

Upper Right:
SHORTLY BEFORE IMPACT

Left:
FOLLOW THROUGH

TWO FAMOUS BRITISH PLAYERS, BOTH SURREY AND ENGLAND

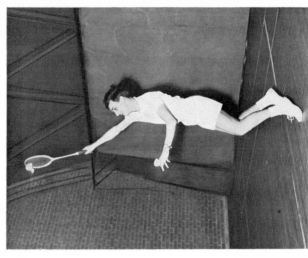

MRS. E. I. TIMPERLEY

E. I. TIMPERLEY

back over shoulder and remain
flexible at the waist.

3. Not watching the
shuttle.

Correction: most players deny
that they do not watch the shuttle
but there is little doubt that it is
the cause of at least half the mis-
hits. Correct by watching the
shuttle all the time, off your
racket, on to your opponent's, off
your opponents, back on to your
own—and see if you can read the
maker's name inside the shuttle as
it leaves on its return flight!

4. Angling the
racket.

Correction: make sure you have
the right grip and that your footwork is approximately correct for
the stroke you are making.

Back Court Faults.

1. Lack of Power.

Correction: this can only be developed by practice. Throw the
head of the racket at the shuttle ...
reach up (and forward where possible) to the shuttle when clearing
... do not try to smash a shot
which has passed over your head,
rather hit it back upwards as a
deep clear.

2. Wrong Footwork.

Correction: check to see that your
right foot is well across your body
for backhands and that your left
foot is in advance of your left for
forehand power strokes.

3. Loss of position.

Correction: remember at all times that your opponents are (a) trying to move you around (b) trying to get you out of the way to leave the court clear. You will counter by playing returns which prevent them moving you around and re-gaining your pivot position—the centre of the court in singles and mixed doubles—with the least possible delay.

Net faults.

1. Taking backswing.

Correction: resist the temptation to take back your racket at all, other than cocking the wrist, when playing net shots. When you do, the shuttle is past you or has fallen, before you can bring your arm back again.

2. Taking shuttle too low.

Correction: make yourself "go for" the shuttle as it is passing the net cord. The earlier the better ... the higher you take it the better . . . this denies your opponents time and means. You have only to topple the shuttle back over, with little stroke to make and therefore less room for error.

3. Not covering the net.

Correction: make the spot just in front of the intersection of the short service line and the centre line your base . . . it is barely a stride in either direction with outstretched arm and racket to give you full court coverage.

4. Playing with a bent arm.

Correction: loosen grip, ensure that even if your natural stroke involves a bending of the arm, the arm is straight at the moment of impact.

5. Not being at the right place at the right time.

Correction: develop your anticipation by trying to work out what will be the *most likely* reply to your stroke—and imperceptibly preparing to move in that direction . . . by getting off your heels, poised to move in any direction at short notice.

Serving Faults.

1. Hurrying Service.

Correction: be determined to pause before striking the shuttle— if necessary by counting up to five.

2. Lofting low serve.

Correction: continue to practise over the dining-room table if necessary. In play begin serving low and work upwards until the shuttle just clears the net.

3. Serving to mid-court.

Correction: determine to serve low or really deep. If you find you cannot get either stroke at first, stand a yard nearer the sideline and angle on to your opponents backhand (from the right court).

| 4. Disclosing your Intention. | Correction: use the same preparatory actions for all your serves, but alter your position occasionally for deceptive purposes ... but bear in mind that as you move out to the sideline, you leave a gap between you and your partner. |

Faults in receiving service.

1. Not Rushing Service.	Correction: remember that this is a fundamental of attack in mixed doubles and all other forms of the game. The loose serve *must* be rushed. It is, after all, a gift. Take it.
2. Wrong position.	Correction: make sure you are ready to dive for the angled serve, pounce on the short service and pivot back for the lob serve ... all can be reached if you are in a state of readiness in an up-court crouching position.
3. Low Racket.	Correction: your racket should be held with the head up at about shoulder level ... this will save a precious split second if you are rushing the service.

General Fitness

It is true that many people take up a sport to *keep* fit. You will get little pleasure out of any strenuous sport unless you are reasonably fit when you begin to play it. This is particularly true in badminton. So much of the play is overhead, so many shots have to be reached for with the foot movements involving twisting and turning to a remarkable degree.

To be fit for badminton is no different from being fit for any game of movement. I can only suggest therefore a few lines of approach for those who feel they are not toned up enough to execute on the court all we have been suggesting.

Take footwork, for example. If you are not over-nimble, you can improve this simply by skipping. A piece of the old clothes line will be sufficient for you—and if you are not averse to taking advice from the young, the little girl next door will show you all the variations with a rope that you need.

If you find difficulty in getting *down* to the shuttle for the low shots you are sometimes required to pick it up off the floor, the simplest exercise in the world will remedy this. Simply touch your toes about 20 times in the bathroom every morning. If you persevere with this, without "kidding" yourself at all or cheating in any way, you will soon find you can get down to the shuttle just as easily as you do to your toes.

But I am non-expert in these matters. If we are serious in our intention to teach ourselves such a strenuous sport as badminton and, having taught ourselves, wish to play *better* badminton, then we must knuckle down to it. The following are some comparatively simple exercises "prescribed" especially for badminton players by an old friend of mine, W. L. Steel, Lecturer in the Department of Physical Education at Manchester University.

Try them to-day. Now? Yes, now! They should all be done *not* slowly but at optional speed.

Exercises.

1. For wrists.

    (*a*) Attach string and weight to pole or old racket

shaft. Take in right hand. Now roll up weight by rotation of wrist only. Repeat 10 times in all. Rest. Do a further 10 wind-ups. Rest. Do a further 10 wind-ups. This will total 3 × 10 repetitions. Now increase weight (essential) and repeat exercise.

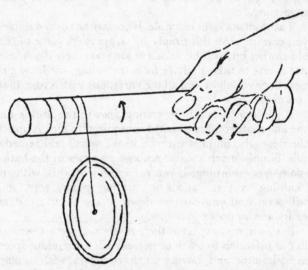

FIG. 20. Wrist exercise. The weight is raised and lowered by turning rod.

(b) Support right forearm at edge of table while holding a weight (a book will do; an old racket is better since you can tape additional weights to it to increase load). Now roll wrist clockwise, then anti-clockwise. Make this 3 × 10 repetitions, as above.

(c) Lie face downwards on floor preparatory for press-ups. But use finger-tip support only. Arms bend and stretch. Raise foot position to increase load.

(d) Carry a ball of paper or a rubber ball with you at all times. Squeeze ball in hand at frequent intervals throughout day. (You can do this one on the way to work, at work and coming home from work).

2. For Legs.

(a) Squat jumping. Knees bend followed by vertical jump high in air, down to bend and repeat without stopping until reasonably tired. Try to increase height or number of jumps per session of exercise.

(b) As in (a) but use a medicine ball or some other weight held above your head as a resistance. Do 3 × 10 repetitions.

(c) Skipping, with straight arms, *using wrist action only*, for turning the rope. This is an ideal exercise for both legs and wrists.

(d) With toes supported on a platform, raised and 1″ thick, lower and raise heels while supporting a weight on your shoulder. Do this a number of times with toes forward, inward and outward, in turn.

(e) One leg step-up. With one foot on the ground and one on the edge of your dining-room or kitchen table, step up and down on to table, *using leg drive from table-supported leg only*. You may not find this easy at first—but persevere and you will feel the benefit.

3. For Trunk.

Trunk movements are included in exercises 1c, 2b, 2c and 2e. Two good additional exercises are:—

(a) Lie down on floor, flat on your back, sit up and lie down several times. Now increase the effect by lying on an inclined plane, with feet higher than the head.

(b) Lie on your back, with arms sideways at shoulder level and legs apart. Now sit up to touch left foot with right hand: lie down again: sit up to touch right foot with left hand: lie down, raise left foot with leg straight to touch right hand still on floor: repeat with right leg. (Here you have two exercises in one).

That's enough for one day. If you have run through them properly, you will have had enough for the moment. Repeat to-morrow!

If you aspire to better badminton, smoking and drinking will need to be drastically cut or eliminated altogether. But if you indulge in either, regularly, I do not recommend sudden elimination. This can sometimes do more harm than good. Your system needs gradual changes of this nature, not shock tactics. Cut down: do not cut out.

Outdoor Badminton

Open air badminton is more the rule than the exception in Malaya and the other Far Eastern badminton-playing countries. It is also widely played both in America and in Europe where the climate is no better than our English climate but where the weather is most definitely superior. Indeed, in Austria and mid-Europe, it has been the outdoor game which has given birth to the more orthodox indoor variety we have been learning.

Can outdoor badminton be played in England? I see no reason why not. My parents played in my youth. One of my happiest childhood memories is of lying in bed listening to the shuttle being struck. Occasionally I saw it float into the air within my view. Patiently I waited for another glimpse of it and secretly planned how hard I would hit it and with what purpose when I was old enough to be allowed to play.

Old net posts can be bought from a club without difficulty or improvised: and plastic shuttles can be used. All you have to do is to wait for that still weather. Then out with the equipment and on with the game. But I do advise using old rackets, as outdoor shuttles are very hard on anything approaching tournament stringing.

These outdoor sets, complete, can be bought quite cheaply from the stores or ordered through your local sports shop. You may find it more convenient when playing leisurely summer badminton to score 21 points up. This you will find is permitted by the Rules of the game (Law 7).

CHAPTER XI

TOURNAMENT PLAY AND TOURNAMENTS

It is my hope that you will be able to learn to play sound badminton from this book. You cannot learn tournament or match play other than by experience. But there are some simple lessons easily absorbed. As F. N. S. Creek has said in "Teach Yourself Lawn Tennis", a companion volume to this: "We are all of us bound to be beaten by good shots sometimes, or to hit (the ball) into the net or out of court—but mistakes of intelligence rather than of skill should usually be avoidable."

Badminton is similar to tennis in that it requires intelligence and determination when played seriously. Badminton also requires a high degree of anticipation and a certain zest for deceiving your opponent. To win a match by fitness and "guts" is rewarding. To win it by outwitting an opponent who has more of these attributes than you, by using more intelligent tactics, is even more satisfactory.

When you enter for your first tournament, you will sooner or later find yourself up against a player with a slight superiority of skill in the playing of the actual strokes. This need bother you not at all. If you use the right tactics—the play that does *not* suit him—you can win. Most top-flight players work this sort of thing out to a nicety; the Oon brothers both make this positive approach to the game.

You should reason like this. "I am playing that former international Kurt Wissel in the next round. Now Kurt is much older than I am. I can afford to wait, making long rallies in the first game to sap his stamina. Therefore I will start by playing all safe, defensive shots.''

I have seen clever players put this sort of plan into effect. An older experienced opponent is nonplussed for a start. He had expected a fast attack and had his defensive play all keyed up. The attack does not come, the rallies go on seemingly for ever—until *he* makes a mistake. The old campaigner begins to get rattled. Well, he says to himself, if this youngster is not going to attack, then I will. He does so. This is just what the young fit player wants, for it is sapping the older player's energies faster than ever. The youngster wins the first game, 15-9, mainly on his opponent's errors. They change ends. Suddenly, the younger man switches his tactics. Without any warning, he begins to play an all-out fast, attacking game, thunder and lightning almost, coming from his racket. The older player is now taken off guard, error is piled on error and he has not the reserves of energy left to mount any sort of counter-attack himself. The young player walks off the court, comparatively fresh, as the umpire calls the score, 15-9, 15-0.

You make your first assessment of your opponent either before the match, from known characteristics, or, if a complete stranger, during the knock-up and the first half-dozen rallies. You make your re-appraisal after the first game. If you have won it comparatively easily on the tactics you had planned, you will, of course, continue. Do not change a winning game. On the other hand, if you are playing your usual game and getting nowhere, you must at all costs change your game. If your opponent appears to be enjoying taking your smashes—intended to be lethal—then deny him the pleasure from then on. Toss up a few mid-court shots of low trajectory and see if he does any damage with those. But again, he may be a player with exquisite drop shots near to the net. You will deny him the opportunity of executing them by deep clearing to the base line. If he is none too fleet-of-foot, you will make him run: if he is very fast, you will try to wrong-foot him, get him moving fast but in the wrong direction.

It is worth bearing in mind at all times that there is only *one point*—one, no more, no less—that decides the result of the match. It is that last point you need to win. All that goes before is but the means towards that end, that one point. That is why you must not get discouraged if the earlier run of the play goes against you. It does even in the best circles.

A good example of this tactical approach to the game was the final of the All-England singles championship at Wembley in 1958. Two Danes, Finn Kobbero and Erland Kops, clashed, as they had done the previous year in the semi-final of the championship, with the same result. This was a win for Kops, rated by most well below Kobbero, a badminton genius possessing every stroke in the book and one or two others besides.

In the first game, Kobbero took the lead at 6-5 by virtue of his variety of stroke, steep smashing and high-angle drop shots. Kobbero was then forced into errors. He hit out twice, which contributed to a run of 6 points in a row for Kops. Kops led at 12-9, then, with a brilliantly masked drop, followed by an untakeable smash ran out at 15-10. Yet apart from these two phases, Kobbero was playing the better badminton.

In the second game, there was nothing to choose between the two players up to 7-5, with Kobbero leading. At this stage there were 5 changes of hand without any change of score—a measure of the equilibrium between the two players. Then Kobbero managed to break the deadlock with a beautiful "wristy" stroke. This completely changed the anticipated flight of the shuttle and left Kops standing. Kops then ran into a crop of errors and the game was Kobbero's at 15-8.

At this stage of the game, Kobbero needed to *show* his superiority. The psychological effect might have been decisive. But instead of this happening, Kops began to smash accurately to establish a 6-3 lead. Then he switched back to the defensive. This enabled Kobbero to pull up to 6-all. But the trap was sprung. Kops suddenly began to go all out for his shots, smash following smash. He won a vital 4-point lead. Although Kobbero halted him at 10-6, there were 5 blank hands at this score—the damage was done. Kobbero gained 2 more points but Kops smashed his way out, 11-8, 12-8, 13-8, 14-8, 15-8.

And what has taken you a few minutes to read took two superbly fit Danish boys just under one hour to play. Yet the better *badminton* player did not win. The cleverer badminton player did.

Miracles happen so often in court games that one of the best mottoes you can pin to the mast is "While there's life there's hope". You will, I know, try hard all the time during your match. But it is as well to appreciate that there are some points of the game, certain stages which are reached, when it is absolutely necessary to pull out a little bit extra, try even harder for a spasm.

This is particularly logical in badminton, where only the server can score. If you think it over for a moment, you will see that your extra effort must come in the rallies when your *opponent* is serving. As long as you can prevent him adding to his score, he cannot win. You can win by his errors. If, on the other hand, you put your best effort into adding to your own score, he may be following the same line, be scoring twice as fast as you and he would win. You should be particularly careful not to try out the clever stuff while he is serving. Do it during your service rally and, if it fails, it will not have altered the state of the score at all.

There are at least two other danger points, when you must produce that extra extra. One is when you have reached 14, game or match point. This is the most difficult point to clinch, especially in doubles. The reason is that your opponent has increased his determination and concentration, has tried to raise his game to prevent the loss of a vital point. You have to increase yours, you have to go one better. The other danger point is when you have won the first game easily—perhaps to 15-3. You are lulled into a sense of false security, your opponents may have decided to change their losing game, and before you can say "Roger Mills" (English Junior Champion 1958-59)—you are 6 points down. From this sort of lead, you can say "R. P. Stephens" (English Junior Champion 1969-70)—you are 6 points down. From this sort of lead, but you are also starting with a determination very much shaken. Be wise. After you have won a game easily, concentrate hard on getting a few quick points to keep your lead, moral and actual.

Variation of Tactics

You will appreciate that, as a beginner, you will be concentrating merely on keeping the shuttle in play. But you will soon pass that stage and be able to play to a certain pattern. By constant smashing and fast driving you will—as we have seen—speed up the game. Lobbing and dropping will slow it up. You must make your appraisal early and decide on your tactics. But do not hesitate to change them the moment you find it is not working out well. The day will come, no doubt, when, like the great players, you can play a certain stroke to a player to elicit a forehand smash, which you will be in a position to return as a winner.

As soon as you go on court, notice first if your opponent is left-handed or not, whether he is a hard hitter or a touch man, and if he is at all timid on his backhand. Armed with the answers to these simple questions, you are well on the way to working out your winning tactics.

Rules-of-thumb are not wise perhaps in these delicate matters hinging, as they do on individual habits. But I will risk one. That is that in most cases you decide on a determined, attacking start. An early lead of half-a-dozen points completely unsettles all but the best class players. Only a small number enjoy "coming up from behind" and and are consistently successful at it.

One habit you must develop if you are going in for tournaments is self-analysis. It is important in singles, a necessity for a doubles partnership. Oh! the thousands of club players I have watched who never improve their game, who go on playing the same mediocre stuff year after year. Not because they are incapable of improvement, not because they do not want to improve. No, simply because they have not examined their game, are not honest enough with themselves. If only they would admit that their backhand was weak, their low service too high, their high service too low, their smash too flat. . . . If they did admit it, they could improve these strokes *at once*.

Another worthwhile habit is Concentration. Believe it or not, it is the biggest match winner of all. Concentration enables you to put into effect what you will. Between two players of equal stroke ability, the one with the greater concentration will win every time. Imagine it is 17 all in the third game, with one point to decide the outcome of over an hour's hard singles play, to decide who shall do battle with the title-holder in the final. From an angled return, the shuttle whistles close in front of the umpire, causing him to drop his pencil, followed by his scorebook. The crowd laughs long and loud. He calls "Let", (as one player has stopped playing) gets off the stand, picks up his pencil and score book, apologizes to the players and orders "Play on".

The player whose concentration is broken by that incident has lost the match. However much he "natters" about it to the umpire, he is unlikely to get the match replayed!

Allied with Concentration is Determination. This is commonly called "guts". The player who has this determination starts with a tremendous advantage. The only consolation I can offer the opponent, is that, to quote the boxing tag: "The bigger they are, the harder they fall." This occurs often with the highly determined player. If you can *break* his determination even momentarily, he is likely to be a dead duck. The sort of sequence that can do it is a lucky net trickle against him, which you follow with an incredible retrieving shot and cap with a killing smash.

In case the foregoing is creating in your mind an impression that badminton is over-serious, let me offer this correction. In my view, no badminton is worth playing which is not enjoyed. Certain players visibly enjoy it. Among the famous, Warwick Shute comes to mind in this category. Others enjoy it to the full but not visibly, players such as Colin Beacon, Derek Talbot, Ray Sharp and Tony Jordan. Others yet enjoy it (they say) but appear to be in agony throughout a big match—perhaps it would be wisest to leave out their names. You will spot them for yourself.

But match players of all categories should constantly remind themselves that it is, after all, *only* a game, and that there are spectators. A hard and bitterly-contested final can still provide pleasure to the spectators. It will do this, providing neither sorely-pressed player allows himself to give reign to his feelings, but concentrates on the winning of the game. "Playing to the gallery", for

FERRY SONNEVILLE (INDONESIA)
Taking a low backhand

MARGARET VARNER (U.S.A.)
Finishing a smash

ERLAND KOPS (DENMARK), 1958 All England champion, in play

The Author teaching himself badminton with Heather Ward at the
famous Wimbledon 4-court club

example, is seeking an unfair advantage over your opponent. This is done by clowning on court, by throwing your racket about, or by exchanging witticisms with spectators or officials. Avoid this kind of exhibitionism like the plague. Let your reputation be for your play, not for playing the fool.

Self-analysis, Concentration, Determination—that should be your winning recipe.

Finally, never, never, take it out on the umpire. He is *always* unpaid and is there to assist the game. Nowadays incompetency is rare. But if you do feel strongly that wrong decisions are being made, ask your opponent at a convenient break in the game if he would agree to you asking for a *change* of umpire. Then refer the matter, through the umpire, to the referee.

Tournaments

At the bottom of the ladder is the club tournament to decide on your local champions. These titles rest usually with the same players for many years running. This is because the player with that little extra class has all the answers to his fellow-members' games. And why not? He plays against them week in and week out throughout the season.

Hand-in-glove with these tournaments go the local rallies. These are sponsored by local clubs—usually church clubs—for church funds or for some specific charity. The promoting club provides the hall, plastic shuttles, and tea and prizes and invites two or three pairs from all the other clubs in the locality. Play begins early in the afternoon. Short games of 9 or 11 points are played or sometimes "first to reach 8 points". You play with a different partner each time, often against different opponents. The draw is split into four sections and the winning lady and winning gentleman in each section provide the

four semi-finalists. These play a full game of 15 points
for the right to enter the final. This is staged at the end of
the evening, a full match, best of three games being
played.

The next step up the tournament rung are the handicap
events played in conjunction with the Open Tournaments and Open Championships meetings. In these you
will find the best club players with a sprinkling of county
players, even an occasional champion.

They are great fun as you will soon find if you enter for
them one day. There are often more than two classes for
the mixed doubles. As the handicaps vary from scratch
to plus 6 even in class 4, you will see that they cater for
the very widest variations in standards of play. At plus
6 in class 4 you will be a long way off the champions—but
you will be playing in the same tournament on the same
courts with the same shuttles. It's a grand feeling and
gives a fillip to your badminton-playing.

The handicap events are usually confined to doubles
play. Where there are singles events other than the Open
ones, they are usually what is known as "restricted". The
form of restriction can vary. Once a year each major
county holds its Restricted tournament, including singles.
Here the restriction is that you have to be a member of
that county to compete. Another type is a restriction to
players "who have not previously won an open tournament or played for their county". I have enjoyed playing
in these and can thoroughly recommend them for young
players.

From these you will step on to the last rung of the
tournament ladder, the "Opens". There are over 30 of
these meetings, one almost every weekend of the season.
Many involve a great deal of travelling, but there will
be a dozen or so in reach of your home between October
and April. Those held at places like Eastbourne, Little-

hampton, Portsmouth, Harrogate, Herne Bay, the Isle of Wight and the Channel Islands, often attract players who combine a winter holiday or long week-end with badminton in congenial surroundings.

The number of open tournaments on the Continent is increasing, too. Not many years ago, there were only the Danish, Swedish and French Championships, the last-named of a much lower standard than the other two. Now there are international championships in Germany (Bonn), Switzerland (Lausanne) and Holland (Haarlem); and Austria and Portugal are taking a lively interest in the game. If you do go abroad, be sure your court manners are unexceptionable. However obscure a player you are at home, abroad you will have after your name in the programme either England or Great Britain. And the news agencies reporting staff will send your result and a report back to London.

Your First Tournament

Now you have taught yourself badminton, you must teach yourself to play in tournaments. To give you an idea of what happens, come with me as my partner to an imaginary tournament. It will not be too imaginary, for all the details are as they occur at the Wimbledon Squash and Badminton Club, Cranbrook Road, Wimbledon, where they stage the Surrey Championships every season at the end of February and the beginning of March. Other large tournaments follow a similar pattern, although many seem to take on an especial character, usually the imprint of a gifted organiser.

We can arrive at the 4-court Wimbledon Club by train or by car. As we enter the doorway in the front of the building, we see a shop window on the left, full of all the latest things in badminton and squash rackets, shorts, skirts—and books. Once inside the building we are confronted by a competitors' table at which sit two of the cheerful and willing helpers. Their job is to check in all competitors, issue them with any instructions they require and provide them with a programme. This shows our names and at what time and against whom we are playing in our particular event. On our left we hear animated laughter coming from the bar and the restaurant-lounge. On our right is a passage leading to the changing rooms. Let's have a coffee. We've plenty of time. We are not down to play until 7 o'clock.

We go into the lounge, order our coffee and notice with pleasure the extensive menu of egg dishes and grills. Just the thing—after we've played our badminton. A cheerful, buxom character assures us she will cook whatever we require if we give her 20 minutes notice. We promise to do so. After coffee we go to the dressing rooms and change into our whites—spotless for this great occasion.

Through the central swing doors at the far end of the foyer we can hear the smack of racket on shuttle. Occasionally there is a wail of anguish at a fluffed shot or a mis-hit. There is not a great deal of laughter—for this is a tournament. Entrance fees have been paid (and every one of these includes a levy to the Badminton Association of England) and all the players are determined not to be put out—in the first round anyway.

We go in and take a comfortable seat in a heated lounge, glass-faced and giving us a good view of courts one and two. Sitting back and enjoying good play we nod to each other knowingly: this is the life, we agree, this is how to enjoy your badminton. The club secretary smiles a welcome to us.

Our self-satisfaction is short-lived. An authoritative voice over the loud-speaker system informs us that "Next on Court one, please,"—golly! us! We panic a little, grabbing rackets, towels, making sure we have a handkerchief—only to find that the game on court one is scarcely half way through. We sink back, relieved. But the trailing pair on the court suddenly have a change of fortune. Before we know where we are, the players are trooping off and our big moment has come. Our opponents have collected a match form from another young helper and a further genial character, this time employed by a sports goods firm, hands us a brand new shuttle, accompanied with a few welcome words of encouragement. We must look, as well as feel, nervous!

But there is no need. Our opponents tell us it is their first tournament and we admit it is ours, too. Everyone feels better for the confession. We mutually decide on a long knock-up and nobody seems to mind. Needless to say, we lose the toss. Our opponents choose to serve. As both ends seem as good as each other, we decide to "stay".

After the knock-up (with an old shuttle) we begin our game in earnest. We admit to each other that we feel a bit shaky for the first few rallies. There's so much more *room* than at our local club. There are no "lets" for hitting the bars in the roof or the lights suspended over the court. Very distracting. But very nice, too, to be able to execute defensive clears to get oneself out of trouble. All four of us "wood" a lot in these opening rallies. I belt every other shot miles out of court. Have patience with me, partner. I shall settle down—I hope.

And sure enough I do. We all do. The score is ten all in the first game and we are all playing our natural game and enjoying every minute of it. You are sweating a bit so you take off your pullover. We all follow suit.

We run out at 15-10, thanks to your good low serving, partner. Keep that up and we can't lose. But, oh dear! Perhaps we have been over-confident. Perhaps we relaxed. We are now trailing 4-9 in the second game and our opponents are hand-in. With a brilliant spell they run out at 15-9. Now battle must be joined with a vengeance. As we mop our foreheads with a towel at the change-over, I suggest we try to speed up the game. Smash and drive everything. The lot? Yes, the lot, I say. We nod to each other. One of our opponents intercepts the nod and looks distinctly worried about the whole thing. I force a smile. Are we down-hearted? Not us, I seem to beam.

It works! We shoot up to 8-2 and have this comfortable six point lead at the last change-over of ends. I told you so, I say to you as we take up our positions, with me serving. Alas! Over-confident again. I serve the hand out with a shot scarcely half-way up the net and they are leading 12-10 without there being any real play in between at all. At least that's how it seems. Now they are leading 13-10. We continue to press hard and maintain the pace. We pull up to thirteen-all one hand down. "Five?" we ask. "No—setting's not allowed in handicap games."

We remember reading that in the rules somewhere but this is a bit of a shock—after that brilliant pull-up too. Our consternation must have upset us. We do not get hand-in again and our opponents run out 15-13 in the third game, to take game and match.

We shake hands with our opponents and thank them for a jolly good game. We have had just on an hour's really hard play in first class conditions. We retire to the lounge and order our mixed grill. We eat it with a famous English international sitting on one side of us, a Malayan star on the other. Later on we go back to the courts to see our opponents get through another round, before they go out in turn to the ultimate winners.

Later on in the evening we watch the finals of this handicap event. This is played on Court Two with an umpire on a tall stand. We should probably have quite enjoyed playing in that match. But it was great fun even to watch it. This is the last of the eight handicap events being staged. To-morrow the five Open events begin. Our competitors' tickets entitle us to entry to the club for the whole week. We decide there and then to come to-morrow . . . to live and learn.

CHAPTER XII

THE WORLD GAME

ENGLAND can be proud of her contribution to international badminton. Although the game was played in a few other countries to a small extent in the early part of the century, it was in London in 1934 that the game was put finally on an international basis. On July 5th, at the invitation of the Badminton Association—formed at Southsea in 1893—the inaugural meeting was held with Mr. A. D. Prebble in the chair. The following countries were represented:— Canada, Denmark, England, France, Ireland, Netherlands, New Zealand, Scotland and Wales. These nine countries formed the International Badminton Federation and adopted the set of rules proposed by the Badminton Association. The Badminton Association agreed to hand over the control it had hitherto exercised to the new body—and put "into the kitty" the sum of £200.

The first President was Sir George Thomas, Bt., the first regulations governed professionalism—and the first "new boys" to join the I.B.F. were India in 1935. Australia followed in 1936, Malaya in 1937 and the United States of America in 1938. Thereafter affiliations to the international body were rapid until in 1958 they had reached 34 national organisations, with 7 temporary associate members.

It is not easy to report on playing conditions abroad; in some cases—China, for example—it is impossible. But the following notes are compiled from authentic reports and from interviews with players from overseas. They will show you that this game you are learning is much more than a local pastime. It was one of the Demonstration Games at the Olympic Games at Munich in 1972.

Australia

The Australian Badminton Association was founded in 1935 and elected to the I.B.F. in the following year. It comprises six State Associations: New South Wales, South Australian, Tasmanian and Victorian Badminton Associations and the Badminton Associations of Queensland and Western Australia.

Apart from Thomas Cup matches against Denmark and India, Australia has regular matches against New Zealand for the Whyte Trophy, where the standard of top players is similar. The Australian badminton season begins in April and ends in late October or early November.

One of their best and most popular players, Don Murray, national champion 1953-54, was seen in England in the 1954-55 season. This was during the "Choong era" or his name would have appeared in the record books much more often.

Their best ladies, Mrs. June Bevan and Mrs. J. S. Russell, have not travelled overseas. Australia have benefitted also from the desire of so many Malayans to study abroad. "Fred" Choong, another member of that famous family, Ong Eng Hong and See Chin Leong have all helped raise the standard of play.

Belgium

The Belgian Association was founded in 1947 and elected to the I.B.F. in 1950. The game has made slow progress there, surprisingly enough, and does not seem to have become an all-classes game. The centres are Brussels, Ghent and Louvain, the last named is chiefly an administrative centre but without its own club as late as 1956 when the eight annual championships were held there.

British West Indies

With the improvement of rapid communications, the West Indians' badminton may soon make spectacular advances, similar to those made in the cricketing world. It is played there all the year round mainly on outdoor courts in Jamaica and in Trinidad.

Badminton started in Jamaica 21 years ago in a Mandeville school, 65 miles from the capital, Kingston. The first tournaments were held at Sabina Park, Kingston, and the game became officially organised with the formation in 1937 of the Jamaica Badminton Association. Election to the I.B.F. followed much later, in 1954. The first All-Jamaica Championships were held at the St. Andrew Club in 1953. The singles title was won by a former Scottish international, J. B. Leslie, who made 11 appearances for Scotland between 1947-1952. He and his wife have done much to raise the standard of badminton on the island. They won the mixed doubles title together in 1955.

The men's standard of play is quite high. The Devlin sisters from the United States played exhibition matches there in 1957 and reported that the most promising then were Ronnie Nasralla and young Eddie Ziadie.

Canada

Outside the British Isles, Canada was the first country to form a national association. This was founded in 1921, and she was a founder-member of the I.B.F. in 1935. Canada has produced a number of talented players of world class. Their first was probably Jack Purcell, famous for his attacking game and uncanny accuracy. He turned professional in 1931 after a short period in the top

bracket as an amateur. Of latter years, Canadian players
have been regular visitors to the All-England championships, and some have done very well, most gaining
seeded positions in the draw and several justifying them.
It was Mrs. Walton Jnr. who surprised English players
by winning the All-England Championship unexpectedly
in 1939. Since then we have seen Marjory Shedd, Mrs.
Warren and Jean Waring (now Mrs. Folinsbee) over
here, and at various times R. E. Birch, Don Smythe, Bud
Porter, Dave McTaggart, Beverley Westcott and Peter
Ferguson.

As in Australia, distance must be no object to the keen
badminton player. British Columbians frequently send
their players over 2,000 miles to play in Montreal and
Ottawa!

Denmark

The Dansk Badminton Forbund was founded in 1930
and was a founder-member of the I.B.F. The Association
consists of six affiliated provincial associations, the
Kobenhavns Badminton Kreds being the largest. Their
multi-court clubs with heated lounges, showers and
restaurants, are the envy of all badminton players who
have visited them. Among the most famous—in Copenhagen alone—are the Amager, Kobehavn, Skovshoved
and Charlottenlond Klubs, all with five courts, the
Gentofte with seven courts and the more exclusive
Valby, with two courts. These are referred to customarily
by their initials, the A.B.K., the K.B.K., the S.B.K., and
so on.

The Danes first international contacts were made
through the Irish Strollers, a famous touring side of the
late '20's and early '30's. The first official English team
played Denmark in Copenhagen in 1932. We sent our
best players, R. M. White, R. C. F. Nichols, Leonie

Kingsbury and Betty Uber, with Sir George Thomas as non-playing captain. England won 5-0, but found the Scandinavians enormously enthusiastic and capable of great improvement.

The sign of their improvement began to show at the last All-England Championships before the Second World War, held for the last time at the Royal Horticultural Hall, Westminster, in 1939. Tage Madsen, who won all three Danish National Championships before he was out of his 'teens was sent to the All-England in both 1938 and 1939. In 1938 he lost to a compatriot, Jasper Bie, but in 1939 became the first non-British winner of the title.

Madsen was the first of the "Great Danes" whose names have become so well known to British badminton players. He was followed by Conny Jepsen, Poul Holm, Jorn Skaarup, J. Hammergaard Hansen and Finn Kobbero, with equally impressive lady players, among them Kirsten Thorndahl, Marie Ussing, Aase Jacobsen and Tonny Ahm (née Olsen).

It was during the war that the Danes were reputed to have made their greatest strides. The Germans permitted badminton to be played and it became the Danish national sport. Now they vie with the United States as top all-round badminton nation. (The Malayans, Indonesians and Indians strength resides chiefly in their men players.) Both with men and women, they seem bound to be consistent winners of the European Zones of the Thomas and Uber Cups respectively. They are great travellers, these Danes, and have played international fixtures against no less than 11 countries drawn from all five continents.

France

Although France was a founder member of the I.B.F. in 1934, the game has relied on a small nucleus of enthusiasts and has grown rather slowly. International matches have been played against England, Sweden and Belgium. Henri Pelizza, the Davis Cup lawn tennis player, was their leading player in the early 'fifties. Their international open championship, first held in the 1908-09 season, has a formidable roll of champions ranging from G. A. Thomas (later Sir George Thomas, Bt.) and Miss Radeglia (1910-14) to Ong Poh Lim (1948-53) and other Malayans.

The game has grown most in the Normandy district, and this area, with Paris, provides the two main centres.

Germany

Germany is one of the later recruits to the I.B.F. Founded in 1953, the Deutscher Badminton Verbund was elected to the international body the same year. There are 8 State Associations affiliated, with the head-quarters of the game at a very fine hall in Bonn. Germany has played England in the Thomas Cup and has played other matches against Switzerland and the Netherlands. The International Championships at Bonn towards the end of the season were first staged in 1955. Eddy Choong won the title on the first three occasions and Denmark is usually strongly represented. Outdoor badminton is very popular also in Germany.

India

India shares, with England, the distinction of being the original home of this game. It is fitting, therefore, that a high standard of play has prevailed there. The Badminton Association of India was not founded until September 1934 although the game had been played for more than 60 years by then. There are now 12 State associations affiliated to the central body and seven countries have been met in international fixtures.

G. Lewis was their first player approaching world class.
He was All-India champion from 1936-1940 and although
past his best on a post-war visit to England, was plainly
an aggressive player with many fine strokes. Devinder
Mohan, Prakash Nath, N. M. Natekar and T. N.
Seth have also played in England with good results
and the Indian ladies Uber Cup team played Cup
matches at Eastbourne and Lytham, Lancs. They
competed in the All-England but none survived the
second round.

Indonesia

Indonesian badminton is of a late vintage, but
threatens Malayan supremacy in the Asian Zone. Their
election to the I.B.F. dates only from 1953 and the
national body is made up of District Associations, 22 in
Java, 9 in Sumatra, 3 in Borneo and 1 each at Bali,
Madura and Makassar. Two of their players, Tan Joe
Hok and Ferry Sonneville have proved themselves of
world class, the latter with some fine play in the World
Invitation Tournaments in Glasgow as well as in the
All-England Championships. They put out Denmark in
the semi-final round of the 1958 Thomas Cup contest,
then beat Malaya in the final.

Japan

Japan has been playing organised badminton only
since 1947, but it has gained popularity there to an
astonishing extent. They have an extraordinary number
of players and receive large tournament entries but the
standard is not very high as yet. There are over 44 branch
associations and these together form the Nippon Badminton Association, with headquarters in Tokyo.

Annual championships are held and the ninth All-
Japan in May 1956 was for the first time open to players

from overseas. The only international match played up to 1958 was against Hong Kong.

Malaya

Malayan Badminton became organised officially in 1934 and by the time of her election to the I.B.F. in 1937 had attained a high standard within her own boundaries. Play was possible practically throughout the year and there were hundreds of outdoor courts in the Federated States (as they were then) as well as several large clubs in the Crown Colony of Singapore. One of their greatest players, Wong Peng Soon, first won a Malayan title, the mixed doubles, in 1937 and A. S. Samuel was singles champion. A Cambridge University student, H. S. Ong, played several successful seasons of badminton in England and gave us a foretaste of the quality to come.

After the war this arrived with a vengeance in the form of the Choong family, two brothers, Eddy and David, and their cousins, Robert Choong and his petite sister Amy, and a great stylist, H. A. (Johnny) Heah, who later married Amy Choong. British badminton owes a great debt to the Choong family. Eddy with his spectacular, cheerful play, Robert with his smashing and David with his tactical doubles play—not forgetting the clever net play of Amy—did much to dispel the idea in England that badminton was a "soft" game. The Choongs won hundreds of open titles between them: while the brothers Eddy and David were involved in no less than 8 All-England titles in the 7 years they were students here. Wong Peng Soon, later awarded the M.B.E. "for services to sport", usually thwarted Eddy Choong on his All-England visits, but Eddy had his revenge by beating Wong on his very last appearance as an amateur in Malaya.

Malaya won the Thomas Cup in its inaugural year in 1949, beating Denmark 8-1 at Preston, Lancs., retained it in June 1952 beating the United States 7-2 at Singapore, but lost it in 1958, losing to Indonesia 3-6 in the final round.

The Malayan Association consists of 9 State Associations and they are undoubtedly the most highly organised badminton playing country in the world. The wresting from them of the Thomas Cup was a triumph for Indonesia. It could only have been done by Denmark, the United States or another Asian country. Most of their internationals have been or are Chinese Malayans, the exceptions being Abdullah Piruz and Ismail bin Marjan, the latter seen in England at two post-war All-England Championships.

Netherlands

The Nederlandsche Badmintonbond was a founder-member of the I.B.F. in 1934, was disbanded in 1938, re-formed in 1952 and re-elected to the I.B.F. in 1953. The standard of play in Holland has never been high and they have produced no players of world class. There is something of a resurgence there now, due perhaps to the influence of Indonesian students of world class who come to Amsterdam to study. Among them in the late 1950's was Ferry Sonneville. International tournaments have been staged at both Haarlem and Nijmegen. Their best players of recent years have been P. Bosman, L. Verhief, B. Loo and Mrs. A. W. Koch.

New Zealand

New Zealand, proud to be founder-members of the I.B.F. in 1927, have 19 affiliated provincial associations, the highest standard being attained in Southland, Auckland, Otago and Wellington. Miss Nancy Fleming,

1938 lady champion has been seen playing in England, as well as two top-class exponents of the game Jeff Robson and his wife Heather (formerly Miss Redwood), who played throughout the 1953/54 season with great success (Jeff Robson's again blunted somewhat by the remarkable prowess of Malayan students). Robson first came to the front in 1948 and has remained in Australia's top bracket for a clear decade, also representing his country at lawn tennis in the Davis Cup during that period. Not yet seen overseas are the famous Skelt brothers; but Miss Sonia Cox, 5 times champion, played lawn tennis in England in 1958.

It is difficult for Britons to appreciate the travelling distances involved for players in this part of the world. It is not at all uncommon to be asked to travel 700 miles for a championship.

This country also suffers from a shortage of suitable halls. The best are at Feilding (Manawatu), Palmerston North and Invercargill.

Pakistan

Pakistan badminton is not as strong as India's and is based chiefly on Lahore. Elected to the I.B.F. in 1953, there are 4 provincial associations, East Pakistan, Lahore, Karachi and Sind-Khaipur-Hyderabad Divisions B.A.

South Africa

The South African Badminton Union, founded in 1939 and elected to the I.B.F. during the following year, includes the Cape, the Transvaal, Orange Free State and Natal, the Union and also both Northern and Southern Rhodesia. There are 15 affiliated provincial associations, most of which have offered hospitality to one or other of the successful tours made there by the

United States, Denmark and England. There are between eight and nine thousand players in all. Unlike many of the more popular sports, badminton is played only by whites, due partly to the high cost of shuttles, partly to the extreme shortage of halls available to the black population. Even so badminton in the Union is a bilingual game, with "shuttle" for the English-speaking, "pluimbal" for the Afrikaans.

The capital city as far as badminton is concerned is Johannesburg where at the Wanderers Club there are ideal conditions to be found in a 3-court hall built especially for the game. Imported opposition has helped raise the standard of the Union's leading players, many of whom would rank as world class given continuous strong opposition in which to get their teeth. Among their best known players are Gordon Byram, C. J. Read, Ken Brann and Colin Bartlett, who played in England during the 1957-58-59 seasons.

Sweden

Organised badminton in Sweden dates from 1936. It is played largely in beautiful halls with the most up-to-date amenities, provided mostly on a municipal basis. The main centre is, naturally enough, the capital city, Stockholm. There are, indeed, only two affiliated provincial associations, Skaanes Badmintonforbund and Stockholm Badmintonforbund. Their men players have made far greater reputations than their women and have been able to challenge the Danes as equals in this field. Among their great players over the last decade have been Conny Jepsen, Nils Jonson, Bertil Glans, Knut Malgrem, Stellan Mohlin and Olle Wahlberg. Nils Jonson, who became known as the Borotora of Badminton (because of his agility and vivacity on court) represented his country 26 times between 1945-55 and was once a single

point away from an All-England Championship title.
Conny Jepsen (who also played for Denmark) won the
All-England singles title in 1947 but would have been
at his peak during the war years had there been international competition.

Switzerland

Elected to the I.B.F. in 1934, Switzerland's growth
has been slow if indoor badminton only is considered. A
party of British players gave exhibition games there
shortly after the end of the second world war and David
Choong and L. T. Lee (Malaya) played on a number of
occasions in the International Championships at Lausanne. But there has been an extraordinary growth in
summer badminton played outdoors with plastic
shuttles. Courts can be hired in Lucerne for under 2/-
a half-hour session, with rackets and shuttle included in
the charge.

Thailand

The growth of the game in Thailand is similar to that
in Malaya ten years ago. Bangkok is the chief centre.
Her leading players rejoice in such picturesque names as
Suntern Supapantre and Miss Pratuang Pattabongs,
seen in England in 1958.

The Thai people are now taking their badminton most
seriously; and have enjoyed the benefit of professional
coaching from Malayans.

United States of America

Although the American Badminton Association, now
consisting of 17 affiliated sectional associations, was not
founded until 1936, the United States claim to have the
oldest badminton *club* in the world. This is the original

Badminton Club of the City of New York, founded in 1878, and still in existence.

Apart from one match against an English team in New York in 1925, the climax to a Canadian tour, the Americans had little or no contact with European badminton. But we had heard of the prowess of Dr. David Freeman, probably the greatest badminton player since Sir George Thomas, and Miss Ethel Marshall, American singles champion for 7 years running from 1947-53. David Freeman played in England in 1949 and won every singles event in which he entered. He had a truly remarkable badminton career. In 1939, when he was only 18, Freeman was beaten by the Canadian player, H. Pollock. He never lost another singles match. He won the American Championship six times running and once again, on a one-season come-back in 1953 after having had no competitive play for four years. He was 28 when he retired from competitive badminton, after a brilliant career spanning only 10 years. He was a truly amazing player, with superb footwork, speed, anticipation and stroke production. Miss Ethel Marshall was seen over here in 1957, but only in doubles play for the Uber Cup matches. Apart from these two players, others of world class have become regular visitors to the All-England, including Joe Alston and his wife, Lois, Margaret Varner and the Devlin sisters, Judy and Susan, daughters of the former famous Irish international Frank Devlin, All-England champion six times in the 1920's.

The Americans are well organised, as one would expect, and do not suffer from lack of facilities in most areas. They use the military establishments in many cases, those known as armouries. These can often accomodate a dozen or more courts and this allows a lot of badminton to be played without the tedium of waiting between games. They do suffer, however, from the

intense competition from other sports and pastimes and
new recruits to the game are increasingly difficult to
attract. Introduction by parents and relatives remains
the most promising source for new membership to the
clubs.

CHAPTER XIII

OFFICIATING

THE Badminton Umpires Association of England was
formed to give uniformity in umpiring and to approve
umpires suitable to take charge of the larger meetings and
international fixtures. Peter Birtwistle, a former English
international, was the driving force behind it when it
was first formed in 1953 and was its secretary for the
first few years of its existence. He was succeeded by R. S.
Lucas in 1957.

Some Northern and Scottish administrators think that
umpiring can be left safely in the hands of the senior
officials and players without the paraphernalia of a
national organisation. But in the Midlands and South
the Association has gained wide respect for its members
and the object of uniformity is rapidly being achieved.
The Association have Approved Members and Pro-
bationary Members. These include many ex-interna-
tionals and players of wide experience.

The following recommendations were drawn up by the
Association and were revised from 1956-69. They are
here reproduced with due acknowledgment, the copyright
reserved.

General

1. Thoroughly know "The Laws of Badminton".

2. The umpire's decision is final on all points of fact: a
player may, however, appeal to the referee on a point of
law only.

3. The linesman's decision is final on all points of fact
on his own line: the umpire cannot overrule him. If a

linesman is unsighted, the umpire may then give a decision if he can: otherwise a let should be played.

4. Where a service judge is appointed, his decision is final on all points of fact in connection with the delivery of the service as set out in "Service Judge" 27. It shall be the duty of the umpire specially to watch the receiver—see 22 (c).

5. All announcements and calling of the score must be done distinctly and loudly enough to be heard clearly by players and spectators.

Call promptly and with authority but, if a mistake is made, admit it, apologise and correct it.

6. If a decision cannot be given, say so and give a let. NEVER ask spectators nor be influenced by their remarks.

7. The umpire is responsible for all lines not covered by linesmen.

8. The umpire should control the match firmly, but without being officious. He should keep play flowing without unnecessary interruptions while ensuring that the Laws are observed. The game is for the players.

9. When a doubt arises in the mind of the umpire or service judge as to whether an infringement of the Laws has occurred or not, "Fault" should not be called and the game allowed to proceed.

Before Play Begins

10. Obtain the score pad from the referee. Enter up the score pad.

11. Check the net for height. See that the posts are on the lines, or that tapes are correctly placed—Laws 2 and 3.

12. Ensure that the linesmen and service judge are

correctly placed and know their job—see "Linesmen" and "Service Judge".

13. Ensure that a sufficient quantity of tested shuttles according to Law 4 is readily available for the match, in order to avoid delays during play. If the players cannot agree, the umpire should have the shuttles tested, or in a tournament refer to the referee, or in a match the captains or referee. Once shuttles have been found to be acceptable, ensure that they are used unless circumstances alter.

Starting the Match

14. Ensure that tossing is correctly carried out, and that the winners and losers exercise correctly their options under Law 6.

15. In the case of doubles, mark on the score pad the names of the players starting in the right-hand service courts. This enables a check to be made at any time to see if the players are in their correct service courts. If during the game the players get in their wrong service courts unnoticed, so that they have to stay wrong—Law 12—amend the score pad accordingly.

16. When the players have finished warming-up, announce:—

    (a) In a tournament:—

        1. "Final or semi-final of . . ." If neither, say nothing.

    (b) In a tournament or match:—

        1. Names of players with country, county or club where applicable.

        2. Name of the first server, and, in the case of doubles, of the receiver.

        3. To start the match, call "Love all, play".

The Match

17. Mark the score pad as the match proceeds.

18. Call the score:—

   (a) Always call the server's score first.

   (b) Singles—when a player loses his service, call "Service over" followed by the score in favour of the new server.

   (c) Doubles—at the beginning of a game call the score only, and continue to do so as long as the first player serves. When the right to serve is lost, call "Service over" followed by the score in favour of the new server. In that and subsequent innings, when the first server loses his right to serve, call the score followed by "Second server". Continue this as long as the second player serves. When a side loses the right to serve, call "Service over" followed by the score in favour of the new server.

   (d) When a side reaches 14, or in the case of ladies' singles 10, call on the first occasion only "Game point" or "Match point". If a further game or match point occurs after setting, call it again on the first occasion. "Game point" or "Match point" should always immediately follow the server's score where applicable, and precede the receiver's score.

   (e) When the shuttle falls outside a line for which the umpire is responsible in the absence of a linesman, call "Out" before calling the score.

19. See that no unnecessary delay occurs, or that the players do not leave the court without the permission of the umpire—Law 22.

20. If an unavoidable hold-up occurs in a match,

record the score, server and the correct service courts of the players on the score pad.

21. If a shuttle or other object not connected with the match in progress invades the court or its environs, "Let" should be called.

22. Look out for:—

(a) Faulty serving if there is no service judge. It is difficult to detect from the chair "serving above the waist," or "racket head above the hand". If there is any doubt, caution the player and ask for a service judge.

(b) The server having both feet on the floor in a stationary position INSIDE the service court when the shuttle is struck, and that there is no feint—Law 14 (d) and Interpretation 1. This should be the responsibility of the service judge if available.

(c) The receiver having both feet on the floor in a stationary position INSIDE the service court until the service is delivered, and that he does not move before the shuttle is struck—Laws 14 (c) and 16.

(d) A "double" or "foul" stroke under Law 14 (h). These should be immediately called by the umpire as "Fault".

(e) On no account allow players to call "no shot", "fault" etc. Warn them if they do, as it may distract their opponents.

(f) Obstruction:—for instance, sliding under the net; throwing the racket into the opponent's court; baulking; unsighting an opponent during service. See Laws 14 (d), 14 (j), 16, 20 and Interpretation 2.

(g) Serving and receiving out of turn or in the wrong court. Law 12 should be thoroughly understood.

(h) Striking the shuttle before it crosses the net, and hitting the net with racket, person or dress, while the shuttle is in play—Laws 14 (f) and 14 (g).

(i) The option of "setting" being correctly exercised—Law 7. It is the duty of the umpire to ask the player's or players' decision. Announce the decision loudly so that spectators can hear, calling "Set 2 points" (or 3 or 5 as appropriate) followed by "Love all" or "Love all, second server", as the case may be.

(j) The players changing ends at the correct score in the third game—Law 8.

(k) A player interfering with the correct speed of a shuttle. The player should be warned, and the shuttle discarded if necessary.

The End of a Game

23. Announce:— "Game to . . ." (the name(s) of the player(s) in a tournament or the name of the team represented in the case of a meeting of representative teams) followed by the score and, if appropriate, by "One game all".

In the case of a match in a meeting between two teams, always define the contestants by the name of the team represented and not by the names of the actual players.

The End of the Match

24. Announce the result and score.

25. Immediately take the completed and signed score

pad to the referee in a tournament, or to the captains in a match.

Service Judge

26. If only one is appointed, he should sit on a low chair by the net post preferably opposite the umpire, but on the same side as the umpire if circumstances so dictate. If two are appointed, each should sit on a low chair behind the back boundary line, or in accordance with the directions of the umpire.

27. The service judge, where only one is appointed, or the service judge on the server's side of the court when two are appointed, is responsible for seeing that the server:—

(a) Until the shuttle is struck, has some part of both feet in a stationary position on the floor INSIDE the service court—Law 16 and Recommendation 32—and does not feint— Law 14 (d) and Interpretation 1.

(b) At the moment of striking the shuttle does not have ANY part of the head of the racket above ANY part of the hand holding the racket— Law 14 (a) (see Diagram)—and does not have any part of the shuttle above his waist—Law 14 (a).

28. If the server does not comply with all of 27 the service judge responsible should immediately call "Fault" loudly and ensure that the umpire hears him.

Where two service judges are appointed the one on the receiver's side should be made responsible for calling "Fault" for infringement of Law 16 on the part of the receiver. He should call "Fault" loudly and ensure that the umpire hears him.

In addition this shall not preclude the umpire also from faulting the server or receiver.

Linesmen

29. A linesman is entirely responsible for his line. If the shuttle falls out, no matter how far, call "Out" promptly in a clear voice loud enough to be heard by the players and the spectators, and at the same time signal by extending both arms horizontally so that the umpire can see clearly. If the shuttle falls in, say nothing. If unsighted, inform the umpire immediately.

30. Linesmen should be cited on chairs in prolongation of their lines at the ends of the court and at the side opposite to the umpire.

31. If three linesmen are available, two should take a back boundary line and (in doubles) long service line each, the third the sideline furthest from the umpire.

If further linesmen are available, they should be used according to the umpire's preference.

32. In response to a request for clarification of Law 16, it has been ruled that the points raised do not constitute a breach of the Law.

The questions asked were:—

(a) In view of the fact that part of this Law reads:—
"Some part of both feet of these players must remain in contact with the ground in a stationary position till the service is delivered":— does this mean that the same part of a foot must remain in contact with the ground, or could it be a different part of the same foot?

(b) If the back foot of a server starts with the toe and heel in contact with the ground, and rises on to the toe as the service is struck, with the heel rising straight, is this in order?

(c) If, on the other hand, the heel comes off the

ground and swivels through an angle of 90 degrees, as is frequently done, which means that the part of the toe remaining in contact with the ground swivels and moves, is this correct?

Accordingly, players should NOT be faulted for these actions.

The Badminton Umpires' Association also adds "Hints For Umpires", one of the most important being the one referring to Law 14 (h)—"This Law now provides that a double-hit is no longer a fault. It is still a fault, however, if the shuttle is hit twice by the same player with two strokes or if it is held on the racket, (i.e. caught or slung)."